Praise for *Everyd...*

With keen biblical insight and insp... ...y ... . g.... .. a much-needed vision for what it might look like to live as faithful followers of Jesus in the modern West. This book will shake you up and push you out into the world with gospel-centered truth and love. Grab a copy for yourself and for a friend and take your revolutionary marching orders.

—DR. REBECCA MCLAUGHLIN,

author, *Confronting Christianity:*
12 Hard Questions for the World's Largest Religion

Pastors face complex cultural challenges within our communities and even within the walls of the church. We no longer have the privilege of assuming that cultural values will align with biblical norms, historic Christian doctrines, and the essential truth claims of Scripture. J. D. Greear's *Everyday Revolutionary* is a vital resource for Christian leaders to boldly proclaim the gospel of Jesus Christ without compromise while still keeping the door open for reaching every member of our community with grace and truth.

—JONATHAN FALWELL,

pastor, Thomas Road Baptist Church;
chancellor, Liberty University

J. D. Greear has given us a great tool for navigating life in our increasingly post-Christian world. His extraordinary confidence in the gospel of Jesus Christ has given him an incredible generosity of spirit that shines through every page. Here is a model for how to love our Lord and our neighbors in a bold, winsome, and ultimately powerful way.

—JOHN W. YATES III,

rector, Holy Trinity Anglican Church, Raleigh, North Carolina

J. D. has done something good with this book. With Jesus and the gospel blazing at its center, he equips Christ followers to faithfully navigate the complexities of modern-day Babylon—not by retreating or fighting a culture war, but by living Spirit-empowered, beautiful lives that display the kingdom of God. This is a call back to the heart of Jesus: to make disciples that transform culture through love, not hostility.

—DR. DERWIN L. GRAY,

cofounder and lead pastor, Transformation Church;

author, *Lit Up with Love: Becoming Good-News People to a Gospel-Starved World*

I can't recommend this book more highly. Through this book and J. D.'s teaching, I've come to understand how important it is for us all to be like children of Issachar, who "knew the times," and like Esther, who realized she was made "for such a time as this."

—HENRY KAESTNER,

cofounder, Faith Driven Movements;

cofounder, Sovereign's Capital

J. D. Greear has given the church a bold and timely wake-up call. In a world that's confused and chaotic, *Everyday Revolutionary* shows us how to live with gospel clarity, courage, and compassion. And take it from me, there's no one better to learn this from than J. D. These aren't just words he would write; I've known him for over a decade, and this is how he lives. This book won't just challenge you—it equips you to live on mission, right where you are. Read it, and let it mess with you in all the right ways.

—JOBY MARTIN,

lead pastor, The Church of Eleven22;

bestselling author, *If the Tomb Is Empty* and *Stand Firm and Act Like Men*

Everyday
Revolutionary

Everyday Revolutionary

How to Transcend the Culture War and Transform the World

J. D. Greear

ZONDERVAN BOOKS

ZONDERVAN BOOKS

Everyday Revolutionary
Copyright © 2025 by J. D. Greear

Published by Zondervan, 3950 Sparks Drive SE, Suite 101, Grand Rapids, MI 49546, USA. Zondervan is a registered trademark of The Zondervan Corporation, L.L.C., a wholly owned subsidiary of HarperCollins Christian Publishing, Inc.

Requests for information should be addressed to customercare@harpercollins.com.

Zondervan titles may be purchased in bulk for educational, business, fundraising, or sales promotional use. For information, please email SpecialMarkets@Zondervan.com.

ISBN 978-0-310-36966-0 (audio)

Library of Congress Cataloging-in-Publication Data

Names: Greear, J. D., 1973– author
Title: Everyday revolutionary : how to transcend the culture war and transform the world / J. D. Greear.
Description: Grand Rapids, Michigan : Zondervan Books, [2025]
Identifiers: LCCN 2025010537 (print) | LCCN 2025010538 (ebook) | ISBN 9780310369622 trade paperback | ISBN 9780310369639 ebook
Subjects: LCSH: Christian life | Christianity and culture | Church and the world
Classification: LCC BV4501.3 .G74 2025 (print) | LCC BV4501.3 (ebook) | DDC 248.4–dc23/eng/20250613
LC record available at https://lccn.loc.gov/2025010537
LC ebook record available at https://lccn.loc.gov/2025010538

Published in association with Don Gates of the literary agency The Gates Group, www.the-gates-group.com.

HarperCollins Publishers, Macken House, 39/40 Mayor Street Upper, Dublin 1, D01 C9W8, Ireland (https://www.harpercollins.com)

Cover design: *Studio Gearbox*
Cover photo: *Street Boutique / Shutterstock*
Interior design: *Sarah Johnson*

Printed in the United States of America

25 26 27 28 29 LBC 5 4 3 2 1

These are the words of the letter that Jeremiah the prophet sent from Jerusalem to . . . all the people, whom Nebuchadnezzar had taken into exile from Jerusalem to Babylon. . . . "Thus says the LORD of hosts, the God of Israel, to all the exiles whom I have sent into exile from Jerusalem to Babylon: Build houses and live in them; plant gardens and eat their produce. Take wives and have sons and daughters; take wives for your sons, and give your daughters in marriage, that they may bear sons and daughters; multiply there, and do not decrease. But seek the welfare of the city where I have sent you into exile, and pray to the LORD on its behalf, for in its welfare you will find your welfare."

—JEREMIAH 29:1, 4–7

When the crowds heard Philip and saw the signs he performed, they all paid close attention to what he said. For with shrieks, impure spirits came out of many, and many who were paralyzed or lame were healed. So there was great joy in that city.

—ACTS 8:6–8 NIV

Contents

1. Jesus in the Purple City 1
2. Life in the Margins 12
3. Right Where We're Supposed to Be 26

Part 1: Honor Christ

4. Why Are We Here? 39
5. If You Want to Make a Difference,
   You Gotta Be Different 55
6. Avoiding the Culture War Detour 73
7. Rules for Peculiar People Politics 94

Part 2: Live Quietly (the *Kalos* Life)

8. Creation-Fulfilling 114
9. Excellence-Pursuing 123
10. Holiness-Reflecting 132
11. Redemption-Displaying 140
12. Mission-Advancing 151

Part 3: Testify Loudly

13. Loud Courage 165
14. Loud Joy 184
15. Loud Generosity 192
16. Loud Hospitality 204

17. When Heaven Gets Loud.............................. 216
Epilogue: Maranatha 227

Notes..231

CHAPTER|1

Jesus in the Purple City

For the past two decades I've pastored in a purple city. Raleigh, North Carolina, is technically in the Bible Belt, but we always say it's like the little hole in the Bible Belt where you put the buckle prong. So many people move here to work and study in our tech, education, and medical spaces that Raleigh, Durham, and the surrounding metroplex do not feel like your typical Bible Belt, red-state cities.

The church I pastor tries to stay out of most partisan issues unless they involve issues of clear biblical morality. We want to be faithful to teach all that the Bible teaches, but we also know that if we get labeled "the Republican church" or "the Democrat church," we'll immediately lose access to 50 percent of our mission field. Our typical approach, therefore, is to teach what the Bible teaches as clearly as we can and let members connect the dots regarding which particular policies and candidates best support that biblical idea.

For the past two decades we've managed that tension pretty well.

But for a couple of notable (and important) exceptions.

A few years ago our community was considering adopting a measure that would have sweeping ramifications on parents' control over the extent of sexual and gender indoctrination their kids received in public schools. Not only did this measure undermine what we believed to be God's created order for gender and sexuality, but it also would have removed protections we believe families are entitled to.

1

As you'd expect, emotions around the issue ran high. After a lot of prayer and examination, our directional elder team believed this was a situation where we needed to connect the dots for our members, especially given the amount of misinformation out there and the importance of the measure for the long-term health of our city. So I put out a video explaining what was being voted on and I urged our members to reject the measure.

It went over in our community like a barbecue at a bar mitzvah.

Not in our church—our church members appreciated the clarity. A few media outlets in our community, however, picked up on what I had said and published it. I got the expected spate of angry emails and phone calls, but then one afternoon a box got dropped off on the front porch of my home. The box was filled with tragic stories of gay people who had committed suicide, implying that I was responsible.

The situation was quite unnerving for me and my family. How did this person know where I lived? I had four kids under the age of thirteen living in our home. Were they in danger? After a few days I discovered that a popular professor at a nearby university had expressed her anger toward my public statements on her blog and posted an article that publicized my home address—what the kids today refer to as doxxing. I'm assuming that's how they got my address.

For what it's worth, I've never had second thoughts on preaching anything in the Bible, regardless of how controversial it seems. I'm not saying it has always been easy, but I understand that's the role of Christ's representatives—to declare the whole counsel of God. But had I gone too far on this one in connecting the dots, naming candidates, and mobilizing our people for political action? Had my overt activism created unnecessary obstacles for the gospel?

Maybe you think that even my asking these questions shows I don't understand how dire this moment is.

Or maybe you'd say that if I'm going to be involved politically, I should start by marching against systemic racism or on behalf of the poor.

Both perspectives raise valid questions that I've often asked myself.

My guess, however, is that you've found yourself asking similar questions as well. Maybe it wasn't about whether you should say something from the pulpit of your church, because, well, you're not a pastor. It was whether you should post your thoughts about the president's speech last night on your Facebook wall. Or put up a sign in your yard during election season. Or express your concerns at your next book club meeting about the local school's new transgender swimming coach. Or speak up at the next school board meeting.

Or whether you should include your pronouns in your bio like everyone else at your company is doing. Especially since your company has basically mandated it . . . after all, if you are a "she/her," is it wrong to simply acknowledge that in your bio?

Or is it okay to hang the rainbow flag in your shop window as every other business on your street does as a sign that gay people are welcome in your store? You don't want gay people to feel *unwelcome*, of course, so is displaying the pride flag a way to communicate that? If you don't hang the flag, will you be targeted? Boycotted, even? That's not the kind of attention you need right now. Your business is struggling as it is.

Most Christians I know *want* to be bold for Christ. They want to live with courage as faithful representatives of God's kingdom. But what does that look like in a society where the one cardinal rule is to tolerate and celebrate others? Rabbi Shmuley Boteach, a popular spiritual guru, says that calling someone else's moral or spiritual approach wrong is "spiritual racism. . . . It's a way of saying that we are closer to God than you, and that's what leads to hatred."[1]

Racism? Hatred? Nobody wants to go there.

Is that what speaking up for a biblical understanding of gender and sexuality makes you guilty of?

Are "bold and bigoted" or "gentle and compromising" the only options?

Every week I spend time with sincere Christians who don't know what it means to live as a faithful Christian anymore. They genuinely want to be zealous for the gospel but are turned off by the prospect of being a culture warrior.

I've spent a fair amount of time in consultation with Christian owners of businesses both large and small, some comprising only a storefront and a handful of employees and others stretching across the world and involving billions of dollars. These businesses believe their calling is to offer great products for God's glory. They want to stand for righteousness, but they don't believe it is necessarily their calling to wield their businesses as weapons in the culture war. It's not that they lack convictions on any of the controversial issues; it's just they believe that their calling is to make their "sun" shine indiscriminately "on the evil and on the good . . . on the just and on the unjust" alike (Matt. 5:45), and to do "good *to all*," just like their heavenly Father (Ps. 145:9, emphasis added). And that means using their businesses to bless and prosper both those who share their convictions and those who don't. Andrew Cathy, CEO of Chick-fil-A, said, for example, "When asked about politics, my grandfather would say, 'I'm not left wing or right wing, I'm the whole chicken.'" Christians want to serve the whole bird.

And yet the Bible tells us that in whatever we do, even in our eating and drinking, we should "do all to the glory of God" (1 Cor. 10:31), which means never being quiet in the face of injustice or complicit in the promotion of evil. "*Rebuke* the works of darkness," Paul commands us, "and *do not have fellowship* with them" (Eph. 5:11, my paraphrase). Furthermore, Jesus' command to *all* his followers is to make disciples wherever they go (Matt. 28:19), and "witness" is the primary identity he left us with (Acts 1:8). The Son of Man came primarily, Jesus said, to seek and save the lost (Luke 19:10), and presumably those of us who follow him will have that as our primary agenda as well.

But what does that look like in practice?

What does faithfulness to Jesus look like in the PTA meeting at your kid's public elementary school?

What does it look like at a sales conference where everyone writes their pronouns on their name tags?

What does it look like when you're talking with the next-door neighbor with a sign in his yard about love being love, women's rights being human rights, and science being indisputable?

What does it mean in a marketplace where being canceled might mean the end of your livelihood?

Many Christians feel leveraged as pawns in a culture war they never asked to be a part of. In the run-in I had with the professor, I wasn't trying to isolate, villainize, or threaten a group of fellow citizens, nor was I trying to be a shill for the Republican party. I simply wanted to be faithful to what God says in his Word about right and wrong and to be salt and light in our community. Gender confusion wreaks havoc in our society, and if we don't speak up about what God's Word says about it, who will?

Perhaps you're having similar struggles.

How exactly *would* Jesus live in a purple city?

Welcome to Babylon

Two Old Testament books, Daniel and Esther, were written to instruct the Israelites on how to live in a world where they didn't belong. The context for *most* Old Testament books was the land of Israel. The books of Daniel and Esther, by contrast, tell the story of God's people living outside it, in places where God's name was not known and certainly not honored.

The book of Daniel is particularly interesting. It's one of the only books in the Old Testament, you see, not written entirely in the Hebrew language. The introduction and conclusion of Daniel are in Hebrew, indicating that it was written primarily for Jews, but the narrative parts are in Aramaic, the language of Babylon, because all the events take place in Babylon.

Daniel was part of a Jewish contingent carried into exile by the conquering Babylonians in the sixth century BC. The Babylonians, under the leadership of Nebuchadnezzar, "burned the house of God and broke down the wall of Jerusalem and burned all its palaces with fire" (2 Chron. 36:19). Daniel was part of a special group selected to serve in Nebuchadnezzar's palace to learn Babylonian ways and get their MBAs (masters of Babylonian arts). King Nebuchadnezzar figured if he could get Israel's cream of the crop, they would help convert the captured Israelites into faithful Babylonian subjects.

In this new context away from their homeland, Daniel and his friends were unable to follow some of the divine directives regarding how to live. They could not, for example, follow all the Mosaic laws about ritual cleansings, feasts and holidays, or community structure. Furthermore, Nebuchadnezzar's administration, which they served, was characterized by conquest, violence, and immorality. Daniel had been swept up into a literal Game of Thrones, and he had to figure out how to live as a servant of the true God in *that* context.

The very structure of the book—with the introduction and conclusion in Hebrew and the stories in Aramaic—presents a question to Israelites: You know how to be faithful to God "in Hebrew," but can you be faithful "in Aramaic"?

Is it possible? How can you be faithful to God in a place where the cultural "language" is entirely different from your own? Where scriptural definitions of right and wrong are turned upside down? Where what should be grieved is celebrated, and what is honorable is considered shameful?

Daniel's experience was harrowing and painful, but amazing nonetheless. Daniel brought not one but *two* Babylonian kings to profess faith in the God of Israel. Daniel didn't fit in—often awkwardly and dangerously so. Daniel wouldn't eat what others ate. He stood when others knelt and knelt where others stood.

He was *so countercultural* that he got thrown into a lions' den . . . and yet *so beloved* at the same time that the king whose decree put him there stayed awake all night distressed that he might have lost him.

How do you become like *that* in our society?

My hope is that this book will show you how. How we can live with Daniel's courage and yet be so beloved by our communities that they fear the thought of our departure.

As Marvin Olasky points out in his book *Standing for Christ in a Modern Babylon*, "Daniel, faithful to biblical understanding but comprehending Babylon, is a role model for Christians who want to work in the dominant culture of America but not be of it. Daniel's life was not easy. . . . He had to be bilingual and bicultural, and so should we be."[2]

Like you, I'm concerned about the direction our society is going, but I believe that God has us here for a reason. After studying Daniel in some depth and considering how Peter incorporated Daniel's themes in his New Testament epistle, I'm convinced that God intends to do some profound things in and through us in the coming days. There will be fiery furnaces and lions' dens, for sure. And those aren't fun. But there's also a God in heaven who shuts the mouths of lions, quenches the violence of fire, and transforms the hearts of pagan kings. And you and I have been invited to play lead characters in the great drama. We're called to be everyday revolutionaries who participate with God in making his kingdom known on earth.

Honestly, I wouldn't trade living in this moment for any other. I want you to feel that excitement too.

A Peculiar People

The book of 1 Peter in the New Testament is dedicated to explaining how to live faithfully as an exile in Babylon.

"But I thought Babylon was destroyed around 500 BC," you say.

Yes, but Peter and other New Testament writers use Babylon as a metaphor for the entire secular world after Jesus' ascension. "Babylon" is Peter's nickname for Rome (1 Peter 5:13), and why he opens his epistle addressing fellow "exiles." *Peter intentionally evokes imagery from the lives of Daniel and Esther because he wants to help us live faithfully, like they did, in a world where Nebuchadnezzar is in charge and God's name is seldom, if ever, mentioned.*

Peter was translating biblical faithfulness into Aramaic.

In 1 Peter 2:9 he said,

> But ye are a chosen generation, a royal priesthood, an holy nation, a peculiar people; that ye should shew forth the praises of him who hath called you out of darkness into his marvellous light. (KJV)

Sorry about the "ye" and the other funky spellings in that verse, but I've copied it from the old King James Version because I love that the KJV uses the word "peculiar." Most modern translations have updated the word to "special," but I think "peculiar" may have been more on the mark for what Peter was trying to say.

Peter was trying to show us how to be *different* from the world around us—how to be distinct in Babylon. And I don't mean the Jesus-tattooed, culotte-wearing, bless-you-brother, in-case-of-the-rapture-this-car-will-be-unmanned kind of distinct. That's not the "different" Peter was going for. We already have enough "peculiar" Christians walking around with Christian bumper stickers on their cars and tambourines in their hands, and I'm not intending for this book to produce any more of those. Peter was talking about living with the peculiarity that comes from being an exile, a citizen of another kingdom, in a place where God's name is dishonored.

Peter envisioned us living in such distinct ways, so *peculiarly*, that "Babylonians" can't help but ask what could be motivating us. Peter wrote:

> In your hearts honor Christ the Lord as holy, always being prepared to make a defense to anyone who asks you for a reason for the hope that is in you; yet do it with gentleness and respect. (1 Peter 3:15)

How do you do that? That's what the rest of this book is about.

Against the World, for the World

After a few weeks I reached out to the professor who had published the blog article disclosing my home address and asked to get together for coffee. To my surprise she accepted my request. When we met up, I told her that I had followed her work for years and appreciated a lot of it. I acknowledged that we disagreed pretty strongly on some things but that it felt wrong for her to take our disagreement to the point that my kids felt unsafe.

She got tears in her eyes and told me she was sorry. She acknowledged she had gone too far. She then said something that took my breath away. She recounted a situation from her life that made her reconsider some things about us. She mentioned that a single mother who lived near her had fallen on hard times, and that this single mother had gotten connected to our church and gone on and on about how well the church had taken care of her. She had a tough time reconciling the church she'd written about with the church her single-mother friend experienced.

I walked into that conversation braced for a "you deserve this and so much more, you terrible person" lecture. Now I was looking into the face of someone I could probably be friends with. Someone I was already starting to care about and who seemed to care about me. We hadn't resolved our disagreements. I'm pretty sure she's still vocal in her opposition to our church's stance on these issues. But I think she saw through our conversation that what drives us is not bigotry and hatred but reverence for God's Word and love for people. Maybe, given time and prayer, she'll come to share our convictions. I can hope and pray. Ultimately, I know it's not up to me.

Even so, that experience left a powerful impression on me. I hadn't been Daniel in the lions' den. Sitting across a coffee-shop table from a feisty professor is not the same as staring into the gaping jaws of a feline predator. I did feel confident, however, that somehow, by God's grace, I had managed to establish trust and respect with someone who previously had seen me primarily as an enemy. I think our church's generous spirit, combined with what felt to her like thoughtful, gracious reasoning on my part, unnerved her.

I'm suggesting that there's a way we can live where this kind of reaction becomes, if not the norm, at least not the rare exception. It comes from being an everyday revolutionary—quietly living out the implications of the gospel in ways that testify loudly to the King we serve and the better kingdom he brings.

In the words attributed to the North African church father Athanasius of Alexandria, Christians are an enigma to the world because they are both against the world and for the world.[3] The "Babylons" in which we are placed should have no one who loves them more, even as it's clear that we disagree with so much of what they stand for. At times we'll make them so mad they want to throw us into the lions' den. Even they will be surprised, however, when they find themselves outside the den hoping against hope that we make it through the night.

As N. T. Wright and Michael Bird say, "The kingdom of God is not *from* this world, but it is emphatically *for* this world. The Church's kingdom-vocation is not only what it *says* to the world, but is also what the Church *does within and for* the sake of the world."[4]

"For the sake of," even as we "stand against." That paradox is what this book is about.

CHAPTER 2

Life in the Margins

But ye are a chosen generation, a royal priesthood,
an holy nation, a peculiar people; that ye should
shew forth the praises of him who hath called
you out of darkness into his marvellous light.
—1 PETER 2:9 KJV

"Coming Out" as a Christian

In one of the final seasons of the television show *Silicon Valley*, Richard Hendricks, founder of an innovative tech company, gathers eight local CEOs to collaborate with him in his grand project of launching a decentralized internet. One of the CEOs, Dee Dee, a young gay man who runs an LGBT dating site, mentions to Richard in a sidebar conversation that he and his partner go to church every week. Later, when Richard introduces Dee Dee to everyone else, he mentions Dee Dee's involvement in church and his hopes for what this new site might accomplish. Everyone gets visibly uncomfortable. Dee Dee pulls Richard aside after the meeting and asks why he "outed" him. At first Richard thinks he's being scolded for outing Dee Dee as gay, which seems strange given that he's running a gay dating site. Dee Dee is upset, however, that Richard has outed him for going to church.

Richard immediately starts getting messages from investors that they are pulling their funding because of Dee Dee. Richard is confused, and one of Richard's coworkers explains to him: "You see, Richard, here [in Silicon Valley] you can be openly polyamorous, and people will call you brave. You can put microdoses of LSD into your cereal, and people will call you a pioneer. But the one thing you cannot be ... is a Christian." Richard's cofounder chimes in: "Yes, Richard. While it is clear they are the source of most of the world's problems, even I wouldn't out someone just for being a Christian." Later in the episode, Richard asks Dee Dee whether his parents are okay with his lifestyle. Dee Dee laments, "My dad says my lifestyle makes him sick." Richard says, "Your gay lifestyle?" "No!" Dee Dee shoots back. "He's fine with that. My *Christian* lifestyle. My dad says he just wants his gay son back!"[1]

The episode is satirical on many levels. The satire of the episode, however, highlights the profound change we feel taking place around us. Practicing Christian faith was once considered a positive. Increasingly it's seen as fringe—even dangerous.

The degree to which you experience these dynamics depends, of course, on what part of the country you live in. There are some communities in the United States where it is clearly still a net positive to be Christian. In some places you might find it hard to function if you don't at least give lip service to Christian faith. But for many of us that landscape is changing rapidly.

In 1984, Christian apologist Francis Schaeffer observed, "Ours is a post-Christian world in which Christianity, not only in the number of Christians but in cultural emphasis and cultural result, is no longer the consensus or ethos of our society."[2] And that was in 1984, when Ronald Reagan was at the height of his popularity and Billy Graham drew the largest crowds in America. Forty years later, in 2024, the "consensus" has changed.

Recent polls have shown that only 18 percent of non-Protestants view evangelicals positively.[3] When asked to choose the terms that aligned with their perception of evangelicals, non-Christians most opted for "hypocritical" and "judgmental."[4] In one of those "man on the street"–style interviews, one young adult, when asked to describe Christians, said they are "judgmental, homophobic moralists" who think that they are the only ones going to heaven and "secretly relish the fact that everyone else is going to hell."[5] Nearly 90 percent of non-churchgoing young adults think Christians show "excessive contempt and unloving attitudes towards gays and lesbians."[6]

When I was growing up, in church we used to sing a song called "Jesus Is the Answer." For most Americans today Jesus is not only not the answer, but he and his people are the problem.

I'm hesitant to use the term "persecution" to describe this new situation, especially in light of what followers of Jesus in other parts of the world experience. As I sit in a comfortable coffee shop typing out these words, believers in Asia, in the Middle East, and on the Arabian peninsula face jail or death for sharing their faith. I'd prefer to leave the term "persecution" for them. In the West we are experiencing marginalization, however, and that is no small thing. Marginalization has many deleterious effects, particularly for those trying to make a living in Babylon, and marginalization is often the precursor to persecution.

Outside the Overton Window

Sociologists have long referred to something they call the Overton window when analyzing public discourse. It refers to a set of subjects, and varieties of perspectives on those subjects, that are considered to be within the acceptable "window" of debate. For example, right now discussions about when it's okay to terminate a baby in the womb are still within the Overton window. People often have strong feelings about their answers, but it's considered a subject up for debate.

Overt expressions of racism, however, are no longer (thankfully) in that window. In the 1860s they would have been.

Over the past two decades we Christians have found many of our most basic worldview convictions, which used to form the *borders* of that window, outside it. Christians once sat in the towers of power in the cathedrals of the West. They have now been defenestrated from its windows.

The opening of the 2024 Olympics in Paris featured a live-action depiction of the Last Supper. In this rendition men and women in drag played Jesus and the apostles. Our society now deems scenes such as this to be acceptable public discourse, but the expression of historic Christian convictions on marriage and sexuality is not. As one commentator observed, the Olympic Committee sent a clear message to all traditional Christians: "NOT WELCOME."[7]

In the 1990s, when I graduated from college and entered ministry, homosexuality was still considered by the majority of Americans to be wrong. In the late 1990s, however, societal perspectives shifted and we began to regard sexual orientation as private preference. It's like that *Seinfeld* episode in which Jerry, George, and Kramer all express their discomfort with homosexuality but feel compelled to follow it up with "Not that there's anything wrong with that!"[8] It felt easier, therefore, for a lot of churches to avoid the subject. Many churches in the '90s lived by the "Don't ask, don't tell" motto made popular by President Bill Clinton. *If you won't bring it up, I won't. Let's just focus on Jesus and how he completes your life, gives you purpose, and can fix your marriage.* And many seekers and would-be Christians were happy to do so.

Those days, by and large, are gone. Almost every non-Christian who visits our church assumes that we have "excessive contempt and unloving attitudes" toward perfectly peaceable members of our society. It's one of the primary reasons large swaths of our city will never even consider visiting our church, and why many who do visit assume that they could never be an *actual* Christian, even if they find our weekend services inspiring and uplifting.

To use the taxonomy of writer and scholar Aaron Renn, in the West we have entered the "negative world" with respect to Christianity. The "positive world" was a world in which Christianity was considered a social asset, part of the underlying fabric of civilization (1964–1994); in the "neutral world," Christianity was considered one option among many (1994–2014); in the "negative world," Christianity is considered a social cancer (2014–present).[9] In the neutral world, secular society often regarded Christianity as a mistake to be corrected, an option to be rejected in favor of better ones. In the negative world, however, Christianity is seen as an evil to be resisted or even eliminated. Although much has changed since Renn first named these categories in 2017, they still provide a helpful framework for understanding the shifts.

This new reality is tragic. I grieve it. But it is what it is, and here's the point: *The new reality changes the rules of engagement.*[10]

And that's where Daniel, Esther, and Peter come in. Each of these Bible characters lived, loved, worked, and witnessed in places where their faith was considered outside the Overton window—that is, it was not only wrong but considered harmful and subversive. The Babylonians assumed that Jewish faith led to societal weakness. The Babylonian victory over Jerusalem, after all, was an affirmation that Babylonian gods were greater than the Jewish God. Likewise, the Romans ruling in the first century regarded Christians atheists and anarchists and held them responsible for the increasing chaos of Rome.[11]

Which is what makes the stories of Daniel, Esther, and Peter so compelling.

The witness of the global church has a lot to teach us here, too, since many of our brothers and sisters around the world have been living in environments like this for a long time.

These believers from other times and places show us what faithfulness in this kind of environment looks like. Ours will look a little different from how it looked in Nebuchadnezzar's Babylon. God's character and his moral judgments *never* change, but (as Daniel shows us) faithfulness looks different in different contexts.

Daniel's difficulties started with the new name Nebuchadnezzar gave him. After Daniel arrived in the palace, Nebuchadnezzar, who seemed to have a penchant for long, complicated names, changed Daniel's name to Belteshazzar. "Daniel" meant "God is my judge." "Belteshazzar" meant "Baal protects the king." Every time someone called out Daniel's new name in the palace, they paid homage to a god that Daniel didn't believe in. Every time Daniel heard his Babylonian name, he was reminded that almost no one around him shared his most basic convictions. And yet he answered to that name.[12]

Daniel knew how to obey God in Jerusalem. Could Belteshazzar do it in Babylon?

Who Am I and What Am I Doing Here?

Apparently God knew that a lot of the Israelites would struggle to respond rightly to this new situation, because he warned them about a deadly off-ramp they were to avoid. Through Jeremiah, who lived and prophesied around the same time as Daniel, God told them *not* to work for the overthrow of Babylon, whether subtly or aggressively, or to seek out some secret enclave in Babylon where they could sequester themselves waiting on God to deliver them.

Instead, God instructed them,

> Build houses and live in them; plant gardens and eat their produce. Take wives and have sons and daughters ... multiply *there*, and do not decrease. . . . *Seek the welfare of the city* where I have sent you into exile, and *pray to the LORD on its behalf*, for in its welfare you will find your welfare. (Jer. 29:5–7, emphasis mine)

This was the opposite of either isolation or subversion. They were to *live in Babylon*, to build their homes *there*, and work, counterintuitively, for Babylon's prosperity. Their role was not to be one of antagonistic separation, nor was it to be one of careless assimilation. There are things that the Babylonians did that Daniel and his friends could never do, things the Babylonians ate and drank that they must not touch, places the Babylonians knelt where they must stand, and places the Babylonians stood where they must kneel.

Daniel was supposed to be different—to shine like a bright heavenly star against the dismal backdrop of the dark Babylonian sky (Dan. 12:3). As Daniel lived differently before God, others would see his good works and inquire about his Father in heaven.

He was to live, love, and work in Babylon, but not as a Babylonian. As a Hebrew exile.

Understanding our "exile" identity is key to understanding our role in our "new" society as well. Which is why the opening of Peter's first letter in the New Testament to the scattered Christians immediately connects us to Daniel's and Esther's time in Babylon.

> To those who are *elect exiles* of the Dispersion in Pontus, Galatia, Cappadocia, Asia, and Bithynia. (1 Peter 1:1, emphasis mine)

Immigrants, Tourists, or Exiles?

Let's pause for a moment to think about the word "exile."

Tim Keller says that if you're living in a country you're not from, you can have one of three relationships to it:[13]

1. Tourist

A tourist is just passing through. Tourists have no intention of making a foreign place their home. In fact, they never *really* unpack their bags or form any *real* connections to the new place. They don't buy furniture. They eat at a few local restaurants and see a few sights, but they mostly stay huddled in their tour groups, living in hostels and hotels, speaking their own languages. They complain if they can't find a Starbucks within walking distance. Political or social problems going on in that country don't really concern them, as long as they don't affect their tour. Soon they'll be leaving.

Some Christians relate to Babylon as tourists. Their goal is to stay separate; they feel little connection to the community around them and its problems. They're simply waiting to get raptured off this trailer park of a planet. "Until then," they think, "don't tread on me."

2. Immigrant

Immigrants, by contrast, seek to make a foreign country their *permanent* home. They want to *become citizens* of this new place, adopt its customs, and acculturate themselves to it. "Christian" may be their heritage, but "Babylon" has become their most important identity.

Many Christians adopt this posture toward Babylon. Maybe not formally, of course—they'll always say that heaven is their home, but their aspirations and goals revolve almost entirely around Babylon. Their treasure is in Babylon. They play by Babylon's rules. Their lives are increasingly shaped by Babylon's values. They seek its accolades and leverage their resources to carve out for themselves a comfortable life in it.

3. Exile

Unlike the tourist, the exile unpacks his bags and seeks to make a home in this new country. He learns the language and adopts some of the customs. He integrates his life into a local neighborhood, forms relationships there, and takes on the community's problems as his own.

Unlike the immigrant, however, he doesn't plan to get *too* attached. Babylon, after all, isn't his permanent residence. It's just his host for a while. He looks forward to the day when he can go back to his true home. He may work to create for himself a comfortable, self-sustaining life in Babylon, but he has no desire to store up the lion's share of his assets in this new place. His home is somewhere else.

He's a bit like a traveler with an extended layover at an airport. Airport hubs have those little shops that will sell you necessities at ridiculously high prices. That's because if your plane is delayed by several hours (or even a few days, as has happened to me), you need supplies to be able to eat, rest, read, work, and sleep.

Do you know what you never see in these shops? *Shopping carts.* You don't need shopping carts because nobody plans to stay there permanently. You buy just enough to get by, because that airport concourse is not your ultimate destination. Christians in Babylon know we're here for an extended layover, but it's not the place we plan to live forever.

Exiles pursue neither separation nor assimilation. Assimilation means we gradually start to become like everyone else. Separation means we try to put up as many walls as possible.

I was reared in the separation camp. Growing up in my little independent Baptist Christian school, I heard countless sermons on the verse "Come out from among them, and be ye separate" (2 Cor. 6:17 KJV). We had our own separate, baptized version of everything. We had our own kind of music—music sung in perfect 4/4 time with tight harmonies, no drums, no electric guitars, no swaying back and forth, and some really wily shape notes. We sported Christian haircuts. We wore Christian fashions. Boys wore ties and tucked-in shirts and girls wore culottes and made sure their bathing suits didn't have holes in the knees. We had Christian sports leagues. We even had these little things called Shepherd's Guides, which was basically a catalog of all the Christian-owned businesses in the community. The idea was that the more isolated we were from the world, the more faithful we would be to God. The *weirder*, the spiritual . . . ler. We sought to be perpetual tourists.

God didn't want Daniel and his friends huddled up in small groups in a corner of the palace singing kumbaya and whispering to one another about the looming destruction of Babylon. They were to *live* in Babylon, speak its language, and, in Daniel's case, be called by one of its names; to *seek* its welfare, own its problems, live among its citizens, pray for it, and work for its prosperity. *For as it thrives*, God told his people, *you will thrive*.

Peter summarized exile life in Babylon in 1 Peter 3:15, a verse that will form the outline for the rest of this book, the profile of the everyday revolutionary:

> But in your hearts honor Christ the Lord as holy, always being prepared to make a defense to anyone who asks you for a reason for the hope that is in you; yet do it with gentleness and respect.

His counsel to exiles is threefold.

1. Honor Christ

To honor means to hold in high regard or to lift up. Some Bible translations render "honor" as "set apart." "Holy" in Hebrew is *kadosh*, and it literally means "other."

Peter is telling us to lean into Christ's *otherness* from the world, to lift that up. Our primary concern is showing that our King is holy, different, and superior to Nebuchadnezzar and all his ways. That's our main objective in every interaction, what we're always "solving for."

21

In 1 Peter 2:9, Peter tells us that we are Jesus' "peculiar people." That means in many ways *we'll be weird*. We'll never quite fit in. Because Jesus is "other," we'll be "other," too.

When it's all said and done, that's the one standard by which our success will be measured. *Did we show Babylon that Christ is holy?*

2. Live Quietly

Peter says we should conduct our affairs with gentleness and respect. He also commands exiles to honor everyone, specifically the governing authorities, and to submit to them insofar as our consciences allow (1 Peter 2:16–17). He tells us to do our work with excellence, for both good bosses and bad ones (2:18). He tells wives that they should conduct themselves with a "gentle and quiet spirit" before their unbelieving husbands (3:4). Peter says we should "live such good lives among the pagans that, though they accuse you of doing wrong, they may see your good deeds and glorify God" (2:12 NIV).

This is what Paul meant by "a quiet life" (1 Thess. 4:11 NIV). Peter didn't use the word "quiet," but the concept is there. The Greek word for "good" Peter uses in 1 Peter 2:12 is *kalos*. It's a beautiful word. Literally—"Beautiful" is arguably its best translation.[14] (Several translations render it that way, including *The Aramaic Bible in Plain English*. Aramaic was the language of Babylon, and Aramaic would have been the language in which Peter did most of his preaching.) *Kalos* indicates a quality that makes someone *stand out* with respect to their excellence, goodness, or loveliness. To live in a *kalos* way is to live remarkably.[15]

Peter envisioned us living right in the middle of Babylon in a way that is *remarkably* attractive. So attractive that Babylonians feel compelled to ask the reason for it. Peter didn't envision our peculiarity manifesting itself because of our pushy God talk or because we defiantly correct the Starbucks barista with "Merry Christmas" whenever she says "Happy holidays." I'm not saying you should *never* do that, just that Peter's point was that when we work faithfully, honestly, and *quietly*, seeking peace and conducting our lives with gentleness and respect, our lives will be so remarkably beautiful that Babylonians will feel compelled to inquire about the source of that beauty.[16] The quiet life sets up our loud testimony.

This is what we'll cover in part 2 of this book.

God's plan to change the world through us focuses not on political activism but on his exiles living quiet, beautiful, *kalos* lives, accompanied by clear gospel testimony.

Now, one caveat.

And this is important.

So important that I'm doing three one-sentence paragraphs to get your attention.

We can't *fully* equate our situation today with Daniel's situation in Babylon or Peter's in Rome. That's mainly because we, at least in Western democracies, have the ability to speak into government in ways Daniel, Esther, and Peter did not. And because of that we have a responsibility, as an act of love to our neighbors, to *speak into* our government. To fail to do so, in light of the power we've been given, would be to fail to heed Jesus' instruction to be salt and light or God's instruction to seek the welfare of our cities. And that would be unfaithful.

Os Guinness says that in a Western democracy to *not* contend for God's laws in the political sphere would be a "failure of citizenship," because in our system of government "every American citizen is responsible for every American and the American Republic."[17] In other words, when God sovereignly puts in our hands the power to bless and help our neighbors through the promotion of justice, good laws, and good candidates, and we fail to do that, we are disobeying his command to love our neighbors, to "do good to all as we have opportunity," and to seek the blessing of our cities.

And just so you know, we're not in uncharted territory in this: While it's true that Daniel, Esther, and Peter didn't have the same opportunities we have, we do see them use *whatever* levers of influence were available to them to influence their governments for good.

We'll explore these tactics in later chapters. But for now I just want to acknowledge that we in the twenty-first century Western world have some opportunities they did not, and those opportunities come with its own responsibilities. That doesn't change our *primary* assignment, however: *to show Babylon that Christ is holy.*

3. Testify Loudly

Live in a way that provokes a question, Peter says. Live in ways they can't ignore you, mute you, or turn you down.

We should love, grieve, give, serve, proclaim, and forgive in ways that make people ask what could possibly motivate us. Our unflagging joy in pain, our unflappable courage under fire, and our inexplicable generosity of spirit should reverberate in their ears.

You may think a quiet life and loud testimony are opposites, but they're not. Our loud testimony becomes all the more compelling when it grows out of the quiet *kalos* life. The *kalos* life of ordinary Christians is the key to effective witness in Babylon, the bedrock upon which everything else is built.

The *kalos* life is what ordinary Christians should be pursuing day in and day out, and what I hope to show you how to do well in this book. As John Mark Comer points out in *Practicing the Way*, what grabs the attention of Nebuchadnezzars in Babylon is how regular church members spend their days in cubicles, boardrooms, neighborhoods, public school classrooms, and preschool playdates.[18]

Michael Green, the British philosopher-theologian from Oxford University, suggests that the overwhelming majority of evangelism in the early church was done by *ordinary* Christians, not commissioned apostles, pastors, or evangelists.[19] Ordinary Christians simply lived *kalos* lives, then pointed to Jesus as the reason. Through quiet lives that testified loudly, they lived as *everyday revolutionaries*, and in so doing they "turned the world upside down" (Acts 17:6).

Before we dive headfirst into all of that, there's a word of encouragement I think we need, because shining in Babylon is never easy.

It comes from a very unlikely place: a scared young teenage girl forced into a fifth-century-BC episode of *The Bachelor*.

CHAPTER | 3

Яight Wheɿe We'ɿe Supposed to Be

And who knows whether you have not come
to the kingdom for such a time as this?
—ESTHER 4:14

If Martin Luther, the famous German Reformer, had had his way, you probably never would have heard of Esther. Martin Luther was one of a number of biblical scholars who weren't quite sure what to make of Esther, the exiled Jewish teenage girl who became the queen of Persia. They've suggested that her story, perhaps, doesn't even belong in the Bible. Why? Because it's messy.

Esther's book poses some troubling questions, such as:

Why are Esther and her people still living in the Persian capital,
Susa, decades after God had opened the doors for them to
return to Israel?
Why is God's name never mentioned—not even one time—in the
whole book? Is that some kind of indication of how disconnected
these Assyrian-dwelling Israelites are from God?

To help you keep the timeline straight: Esther's story took place about forty years *after* Daniel's ended. Zerubbabel, Ezra, and

Nehemiah had all led groups back to their homeland according to Jeremiah's prophecy[1] and God's command.[2] They'd experienced God's miraculous provision in doing so. God moved on King Cyrus to pay for a lot of this, and he supernaturally protected Nehemiah during the reconstruction of Jerusalem's walls. Back in the land of Judea there had been revivals in which faithful Hebrews read Scripture over the old temple mound twenty-four hours a day for several days straight.

Esther was part of a group that stayed in Persia, however. And we don't quite know why. Jews back in Judea at the time accused this group of being soft traitors, of getting too comfortable in captivity and forgetting where they were truly from. And, honestly, it's hard to say they were wrong. God had told them the exile was over and it was time to go home. Some may have felt compelled to stay for practical reasons, but it's still hard to understand why so many didn't go home. God had reopened the door to the promised land!

Then, through a series of interesting, if not disturbing, events, Esther found herself as the new queen of this pagan empire. I won't fully go into it, but King Ahasuerus, head of the Persian empire (the empire that took over for the Babylonians), hosted a fifth-century-BC version of *The Bachelor*, and Esther won. If you think I'm exaggerating here, go read it! It's one of the craziest stories in the Bible.

This raises questions about whether Esther should have been in this contest. It was an inherently immoral contest, and Esther had to *conceal* her Jewish identity to enter it. Of course, Esther likely had little choice in the matter, as Jewish refugee girls in the fifth century BC didn't have much agency. Then again, Joseph, a slave in Potiphar's house in Egypt, didn't have much choice when Potiphar's wife commanded him to sleep with her, and Joseph went to prison for his refusal. Should Esther have done the same? Tough questions.

Long story short, after Esther won the contest, her story took an interesting turn. She found out about a plot by Ahasuerus's chief of staff, Haman, otherwise known as the Dwight Schrute of Persia, to kill all the Jews there. Mordecai, Esther's older cousin and confidant, told her that she needed to do something to stop it. Esther said, "But cousin, what can I do? I'm part of a conquered and enslaved people group, and if I try to stop Ahasuerus, he'll just kill me. His ego is so fragile that he had his previous wife banished from the kingdom just for refusing to dance naked in front of him and his drunk buddies! How is he going to react if I waltz in telling him how to run his kingdom?"[3]

Mordecai's response:

"Perhaps you were made queen for just such a time as this?" (Esther 4:13–14 NLT)

Let me cut to the chase: Esther risked her life to save her fellow Jews, and ultimately she prevailed. Not only did she save the lives of thousands of Jews, but many Persians—including King Ahasuerus himself—recognized the hand of God in it all and gave honor to him.

In this instance, I'm glad Martin Luther didn't have his way, because Mordecai's words to Esther have provided a challenge to exiles in every generation, and they are especially poignant in ours:

Perhaps you're here for just such a time as this?

God has us here for a purpose. Maybe the path getting us here hasn't been pretty. We might be tempted to analyze whose fault it is that we are here. But the primary question for us to ask is this:

What does God want from us now?

For what purpose has God brought us into *this* Babylonian kingdom at just such a time as this?

Joining God in What He Is Doing *Now*

When I was in college, I did a Bible study called *Experiencing God* that truly changed my life. I know we throw around that "changed my life" phrase a lot, but this one actually did. I've never thought of ministry the same after it.

The 354-page Bible study really only had one point: God doesn't want us out trying to do great things for him. He wants us to discern where he is already at work around us and join him in that.

The author of the Bible study, Henry Blackaby says,

> [God] does not invite us to set magnificent goals and then pray that he will help us achieve them. He already has his own agenda when He approaches us. . . . We don't choose what we will do for God; he invites us to join him where he wants to involve us.[4]

Blackaby then demonstrates how person after person in the Bible experienced the power of God this way. It's like I heard Kathy Keller, wife of the late Tim Keller, once say: "Want to be a part of a successful church plant? Figure out where God is about to pour out revival and move there about six months before."

Even Jesus understood his ministry as joining the Father where he was already at work. "I do nothing of my own initiative," Jesus said. "The Father is always at work around me . . . and I do what I see the Father doing" (John 5:17, 19, my paraphrase).

The context for Jesus' statement was Jesus explaining to his disciples why he had healed a *particular* lame man by the pool of Bethesda and not all the others. You see, a lot of infirm people were by the pool that day, but Jesus healed only one—the one he knew the Father was already at work in.

Take a moment to let that sink in: *Even Jesus didn't pursue his own initiative in ministry.* His primary question in ministry was not "What would I like to see done?" but "What is the Father doing around me, and where is he calling me to join him?"

Therefore, the question is not what kind of world *we* want to make for God. The question is what the sovereign God intends to do through us—what does he want us to do in this time and place?

Even the best plans, if they are not *God's*, are the wrong ones. That truth is going to be really important as we try to figure out what faithfulness looks like in our modern Babylon. It's not simply about right and wrong; it's about what the Spirit of God is doing.

The place he's working is the place where we'll find his power.

Right Where You're Supposed to Be

One of the things that stands out to me as I read the Bible is that in the worst moments of Christian history God was often doing a different thing from what everyone expected, a *better* thing, even though it wasn't the exact thing God's people wanted.

The early church, for example, under Peter's leadership in Jerusalem, was doing *great*. Three thousand people had professed Christ *in one day*, followed by five thousand a few days later. A large number of Jewish priests had come to faith in Christ. Miracles were happening on the reg. All-night prayer meetings sprang up spontaneously. Every night different groups gathered to hear one of the apostles teach about something they'd heard from Jesus. Believers shared all their possessions; they sang, prayed, and fellowshiped together nonstop. Rooms literally shook with God's power! It was awesome. Sure, the movement still faced opposition, but things seemed to be gaining traction. Momentum was swinging their direction. Imagine how excited the apostles were. *It's finally happening! Jerusalem is going to turn, en masse, to faith in Jesus. The promise of a Jerusalem dedicated to the glory of God that becomes a worldwide center of blessing to the nations is finally being fulfilled!*

Now imagine how confused Peter must have been when a seemingly random persecution broke up this nascent church, brought the evangelistic momentum in Jerusalem to a virtual halt, and scattered the bewildered band of believers all around the world.

Luke, the author of the book of Acts, notes, however, that God was fully in charge of what was happening. Luke conveyed that by tucking a little detail into his description of their scattering:

> And they were all scattered throughout *the regions of Judea and Samaria*. . . . Those who were scattered went about preaching the word. (Acts 8:1, 4, emphasis mine)

You see, when Jesus had commissioned this first church, he gave them the assignment to carry the gospel to the ends of the earth. They were to start in Jerusalem, then move from there to the rest of Judea, then to Samaria, and finally to the uttermost parts of the earth (Acts 1:8). As awesome as those first few months of church life were, they were still only in "phase one" of what God wanted to do. God used the persecution to fulfill his plans, and this group of scattered believers planted churches throughout Judea (Acts 8:1–4; 9:31), in Samaria (Acts 8:5–8), and eventually to the ends of the earth (Acts 8:26–40).

What the disciples wanted in Jerusalem—a thriving church in a peaceful context—was a *good* thing; it just wasn't what God wanted. God wanted to put witnesses in Babylons around the world.

Just as God was sovereign in the stories of Esther, Daniel, and Peter, he's sovereign in our stories, too. He doesn't delight in our pain or misfortune, but he does promise to use it for good. It may not be what we *wanted*, but it will turn out, eventually, to be better than what we wanted.

In this persecution, this marginalization, as we are moved to the peripheries of the Overton window, God is working.

A Theology of Place?

Heather Holleman, a committed Christian and literature professor at Penn State, says that Christians today need to recover a "theology of place." A theology of place, she says, is an awareness that, wherever you are, God placed you there for an Acts 1:8 purpose.[5]

Paul referred to this theology of place, Holleman says, in Acts 17, when he said to a bunch of Greeks living in Athens,

> [God has] determined allotted periods and the boundaries of [the nations'] dwelling place[s], that they should seek God, and perhaps feel their way toward him and find him. (Acts 17:26–27)

In other words, God sovereignly arranges the borders of *nations* so that people in those nations will have the chance to seek him. If God does that with whole nations, Holleman says, then surely we can be confident he is doing that with our own personal "borders," too. God has appointed our *personal* dwelling places so that others around us can hear about God *through* us and seek him *because* of us.

That's how it worked with Daniel, after all. Nebuchadnezzar thought he'd merely conquered Judah. Unwittingly, he turned Babylon into a huge mission field.

You are in that profession, or living in that neighborhood, or residing in that particular hall, or sitting next to that particular person, for a reason. Your successes *and* failures put you into contact with particular people whom God is seeking. Holleman challenges Christians working in secular places to ask the question "What do you see?"

Who is there?

What needs do you see?

What questions are they asking?

What crises are they in?

Where might God be at work?

Wherever you are, God has determined *your* place—the borders of where you live and who you know. He has sovereignly directed the choices, successes, and failures that brought you here. He did that because he's at work in the people around you, putting questions and problems in their lives so that they might seek him. And he brought them up next to you.

Open your eyes and join him.

The Girl on the Plane

A couple of years ago one of our teaching pastors shared the most remarkable story that illustrates how God does this today in things both big and small. He and his wife were hosting his daughter's small group at their house, and he introduced himself to the small-group leader. When he did, she smiled and said, "We've actually met before. We met a couple of years ago in the gate area of the RDU airport, where we were both waiting to board a 6:00 a.m. flight to Atlanta.

"You sat down near me," she said, "and as we waited to board the plane, you noticed I was reading a book by the atheist Richard Dawkins, called *The God Delusion*, and you said, 'Wow, that's a lot of heavy reading this early in the morning.' And then you said something like, 'Are you trying to figure out if God is really there or not?' And I can't remember what I said, but you seemed interested and started sharing your story of how you came to know Jesus."

The teaching pastor hadn't told her he was a pastor, because when people find that out, they get cagey and start apologizing for their French, whatever that means.

She continued, "When we got on the plane, I sat, like, two rows behind you, and you struck up a conversation with the guy next to you. You shared the exact same story with him of how you came to know Jesus, but you went a lot deeper into it all.

"Now, I don't know if you know this," she said, "but you really don't have an *inside* voice, which means you were basically sharing all of this with that whole section of our plane. At this point I was annoyed, because all I wanted was to sleep on the flight—but I'd forgotten my headphones, so I had no choice but to sit there and listen to you.

"When the plane landed, I walked to the other end of the terminal and got in line at a bakery, and I heard someone talking ahead of me, and I looked up and couldn't believe it—it was you again."

She went on, "No offense, but I was so annoyed. But the lady in front of you had two small kids, and she was having the hardest time finding her money to pay, and you said, 'Don't worry about it, I'll take care of it,' and you bought her breakfast for her. So I thought, 'Well, this guy may be annoying, but at least he's not a total jerk.'

"Okay, fast-forward six months," she said. "I'm sharing some of my questions about God with a coworker at Duke, and I brought up to her that I'd met this random guy in the gate area at RDU airport and told her some of the stuff you'd said. She kept telling me she was praying for me and kept inviting me to her church. Eventually I came—I mainly did it so she'd stop pestering me. We sat down, and out onstage walked . . . *the pastor from the plane*. My jaw hit the floor. I said to my friend: 'That's him. That's the guy!'"

Fast-forward another six months. She started coming to church regularly. She received Christ and got baptized. A few months later she joined our high school ministry team, and she now disciples a group of high school girls.

The first time he heard any of this was when she was standing in his kitchen.

Lest you think that this is just what life is like as a pastor—hardly. Being a pastor is usually an impediment to these kinds of encounters. When you introduce yourself as clergy, people get nervous and try to avoid you! These things happen when you are aware that God is always at work around you, and that your job, wherever you are, is to discern where God is at work and join him in it. I like to think of myself as walking through life with a divine magnet in my hand, passing it over anyone I meet to see whether I can discern the "metal" of where he might be at work around me.

As our pastor was doing that at 6:00 a.m. in an airport waiting lounge, someone else at Duke was praying for and working on the same person. And God wove it all together in a beautiful redemptive story that led a wandering, confused young woman to find hope in Jesus.

This wasn't a situation the pastor dreamed up as he left his house that morning, and it wasn't even his preference for how he wanted the morning to go. He'd actually been annoyed, he said, that he hadn't been upgraded to a nicer section on the flight! He had missed being upgraded by one seat. (I told him God had probably sent an angel just to take his upgrade spot so that he could be within earshot of this young woman.)

As Christians we might feel frustrated that we're not often brought up to the "first class" section of society's plane anymore. The "positive world" had its perks! But that's okay. God has us right where he wants us. He has people he's working in whom he wants us to hear from.

Do you find yourself in a situation—perhaps at a particular school, in a particular job, or living next to someone—wondering how you got there? What if God *wants* you there, at least for now?

Rather than resist his will, why not pray for those in your "Babylon"? You never know when you'll discover your heavenly Father powerfully at work.

God has a plan for us here. It may not be our ideal plan.

It's better.

PART 1
Honor Christ

Peter told the exiles in his era's Babylon to "honor Christ the Lord as holy" (1 Peter 3:15).

"Holy" is one of those words that conjures up all kinds of images. If you grew up in church as I did, you might associate it with quietness, reverence, and nasally organ music. In the Hebrew tradition, however, "holy" meant "different," "completely other," or "distinct." It's the Bible's most repeated descriptor of God. Moses used it to describe God more than one hundred times! God is "set apart" by his awesomeness, by his character, by how he rules the world, and by what he is doing in it. His rule in the world and his agenda for it are unlike anyone else's. He's different. Completely and awesomely different.

For us to "honor Christ as holy in our hearts" means that we embrace that otherness. Some translations say that we should "set apart" Christ as holy, meaning that our primary mission is to show off his *distinctiveness* to the world—that is, to demonstrate, in every interaction, who he is and what he's about, or to make sure others see the difference between him and all rival kings.

That's the supreme task of Christians in Babylon, the center of all that we do. That's the *one* standard by which our success will be measured: *Did we demonstrate to Babylon the full truth about Jesus and his saving work?*

In the next few chapters, we'll look at what that means—and what it doesn't.

CHAPTER | 4

Why Are We Here?

But you will receive power when the Holy
Spirit has come upon you, and you will be
my witnesses in Jerusalem and in all Judea
and Samaria, and to the end of the earth.

—ACTS 1:8

A few years ago I was invited with a handful of other Christian leaders to have dinner with the president at the White House. The president addressed us for a few minutes and then asked if there was anything we'd like to say to him. For the next hour it was open-mic night with the president of the United States.

How various Christian leaders chose to respond in that moment was . . . interesting. Many offered words of encouragement. A few gave mild admonishments or suggestions. Some doled out shameless flattery. A couple even seemed to jockey for positions in the administration. Most promised to pray.

Later that night I sat in our hotel lobby with some of the other guests processing the evening. One told me how after dinner he'd made his way over to the president and said to him, "Mr. President, I want you to know that we are committed to praying each day for you." He said the president stared at him for a moment and said, "That's great, but what I really need you to do is get your people out to vote for me."

My colleague persisted and said something like, "Well, of course, Mr. President, we'll do that, too. That's why we're here. But the most important thing we can do is pray for you."

The president, he said, paused for another long moment, then said, "Yeah . . . but what I *really* need you to do is get your people out to vote for me."

I know that's often (sadly) just the way of politics, and I've heard stories like this from both sides of the aisle.

To be totally candid, however, my primary concern is not with what the president said (though it is disturbing). My primary concern is with the unspoken assumption on the part of the president and many of my colleagues that getting out the vote is *why we're here*.

I'm not trying to be too nitpicky about my colleague's words— like I said, I can't remember the exact words—but is that really *why we're here*? Is mobilizing voters to get someone elected primarily *why* God has us here in Babylon, sitting around the table with the president?

Jack Welch famously said that the way to succeed in any organization is to figure out *how* they keep score, and then *score*. Which means that if we want to live successfully as Christians in Babylon, we have to determine *how Jesus keeps score*.

What does Jesus regard as the "win" for his church?

How Jesus Keeps Score

The short answer is that he put us here to testify to his distinct otherness. He commissioned us primarily to be his witnesses, not his political revolutionaries. As I'll demonstrate, that doesn't *exclude* working within the political process to promote justice and seek the welfare of our cities—in fact, that is *part* of our witness—but we're not here *primarily* to establish a kingdom on earth. We influence and shape the earthly kingdoms we're a part of, yes, but our primary kingdom is (currently) not of this world. We testify to it, and give signs of it, but we're not trying to establish it here on earth in its fullness. At least not yet. Let me prove it.

In the final seconds before Jesus ascended back to heaven, his disciples asked him:

> "Lord, will you at this time restore the kingdom to Israel?" He said to them, "It is not for you to know times or seasons that the Father has fixed by his own authority. But you will receive power when the Holy Spirit has come upon you, and you will be my witnesses in Jerusalem and in all Judea and Samaria, and to the end of the earth." (Acts 1:6–8)

The disciples were asking about the timeline for establishing Jesus' political kingdom and what they might do to help bring it about. *That's not your concern,* Jesus said; *when I return is under the Father's control. For now, my power is coming upon you to testify.*

In Matthew's account of Jesus' final charge to his disciples, what Christians call "the Great Commission," Jesus made the same point:

> And Jesus came and said to them, "All authority in heaven and on earth has been given to me. Go therefore and make disciples of all nations, baptizing them in the name of the Father and of the Son and of the Holy Spirit, teaching them to observe all that I have commanded you. And behold, I am with you always, to the end of the age." (28:18–20)

Navigators founder Dawson Trotman points out that Jesus used only one verb in that commission: *mathēteusate*, or "make disciples."[1] In other words, everything else in that sentence that looks like a verb to us (*go, baptize, teach*) is a participle. "So what?" you say. Well, in

Greek, that indicates that the actions conveyed by the participles flow out of, or anchor themselves to, the verb. Everything else we do in the church has as its anchor point "making disciples." All our other activities should be evaluated by how well they help us make disciples. All our "participles," so to speak, flow out of that one central verb.

That both transforms our politics and trumps them.

Believing the Gospel *Transforms* Our Politics

No Bible writer ever said, "Just preach the gospel and don't worry about what's happening in society around you." The prophets and apostles expected the gospel to transform societies. You can see that in how Paul counseled his convert Philemon to deal with his runaway slave, Onesimus. No longer could Philemon treat Onesimus merely as property to be exploited. Onesimus was now a brother in Christ, an equal in God's eyes (Philem. 1:16). *You must treat others*, Paul admonished Philemon, *as God has treated you* (v. 17).

Believing the gospel has profound societal implications. Abraham Kuyper, the Dutch theologian and politician, is famously reported to have said, "There is not one square inch of the entire cosmos over which Jesus does not declare, 'Mine!'" Believing the gospel changes how you see everything—yourself, your world, your neighbors and your obligations to them, even your responsibilities toward creation itself.

Esau McCaulley observes that Bible writers in both the Old and New Testaments never envisioned a Christianity kept entirely in the "private spirituality" sphere:

> According to Isaiah, true practice of religion ought to result in concrete change, the breaking of yokes. He does not mean the

occasional private act of liberation, but "to break the chains of injustice." What could this mean other than a transformation of the structures of societies that trap people in hopelessness? Jesus has in mind the creation of a different type of world.[2]

Indeed. Most of the freedoms we enjoy in Western countries today have come from *Christians who got involved in politics*. For example, N. T. Wright and Michael Bird point out:

Most people in today's world recognize as noble the ideas that we should love our enemies, that the strong should protect the weak, and that it is better to suffer evil than to do evil. *People in the West treat such things as self-evident moral facts. Yet such values were certainly not self-evident to the Greeks, Romans, Arabs, Vikings, Ottomans, Mongols or Aztecs.*[3]

Where did those ideas come from?

From Christians who brought their worldview to bear in politics.

It's true, Wright and Bird say, that "the Apostle Paul did not march around the Roman Forum with a sign saying, 'Slave lives matter!'" Yet the words he wrote in Galatians 3:28, that in the Messiah, 'there is no longer slave or free; there is no "male and female,"' laid the bedrock for the abolition of slavery and the founding of feminism."[4]

Consider this contrast: The first-century Roman emperor Claudius commissioned a statue to commemorate his conquest of Britain, depicting himself, muscular and mighty, raping a young British slave girl. The statue was his boast, his pride. We now find that horribly offensive. Why do we *now* have laws protecting the vulnerable from sexual exploitation when then they celebrated it?

In other words, why is Harvey Weinstein today deemed a criminal while Claudius, who was guilty of the same things, was feted with a marble statue?[5]

Because Christians brought their worldview to bear in politics.

The pagan philosopher Celsus lampooned early Christianity as a detestable religion that appealed to only "the foolish, the dishonorable, the stupid, only women, slaves and little children."[6] That a movement embraces such groups would now be considered its greatest honor. Why?

Because Christians brought their worldview to bear in politics.

Os Guinness says in *The Magna Carta of Humanity*, "The Christian faith made the West, nothing else. . . . Torah, Exodus, covenant [are] behind the notion of 'Constitution.' Consent of the government comes from Exodus and separation of powers comes from the Old Testament."[7] British historian Tom Holland points out that the very idea of charity, a social safety net for the vulnerable, was introduced by Christians.[8] Pre-Christian culture, he notes, had no such model:

> The heroes of the *Iliad*, favourites of the gods, golden and predatory, had scorned the weak and downtrodden. So too . . . had the philosophers. The starving deserved no sympathy. Beggars were best rounded up and deported. . . . Only fellow citizens of good character who, through no fault of their own, had fallen on evil days might conceivably merit assistance.[9]

Thank God Christians brought their worldview to bear in politics.

Countries that adopt a Christian worldview tend to flourish economically, too. Theologian Wayne Grudem and economist Barry Asmus note that the single most reliable predictor for the future flourishing of any society in the developing world has been whether or not they embrace the worldview assumptions of Christianity.[10] Places in the world that have not felt the influence of Christianity are the most behind when it comes to the protection of basic human rights. UNICEF reports that only 24 percent of countries have gender parity when it comes to secondary education, and of those 24 percent, all have a Christian heritage.[11]

I could go on and on. The point is that for two thousand years the greatest moral revolutions in human history have come as Christians proclaimed the teachings of Jesus to the world's Nebuchadnezzars. As the famous Christmas hymn celebrates it, "And *in his name*, all oppression shall cease."[12]

Societal transformation may not be our *central* assignment, but it's the inevitable result of believing the gospel. The gospel changes everything. Indeed, inspiring and catalyzing this kind of transformation is not antithetical to our commission to be his witnesses but *part of it.* The gospel's ability to produce the most just and flourishing societies in world history is powerful evidence of its veracity.

Failing to apply our Christian worldview to political questions has been one of the things that has most tarnished our witness. The persistence of institutionalized discrimination and Jim Crow laws in those parts of the South where evangelical churches were the strongest, for example, has undermined gospel testimony for multiple generations in the United States. Popular media outlets still depict strong evangelical convictions and racial discrimination as synonymous. An unfair generalization, no doubt, but the inconsistency of many evangelical Christians on this issue made that smear all too easy.

In the same letter in which Paul famously admonished Christians to pray for their leaders (1 Tim. 2:1–4), he also critiqued a handful of established Roman political practices, including enslavement and institutionalized sexual immorality (1:8–11). From this observation, Esau McCaulley concludes:

> Prayer for leaders *and* criticism of their practices are not mutually exclusive ideas. Both have biblical warrant in the same letter.[13]

Believing the gospel transforms our politics. That's a vital part of our witness.

But there's a necessary counterbalance to this. Gospel witness also *trumps* our politics. We know that because there are times when Jesus and the apostles pulled back from political matters so they could more effectively preach the gospel.

Preaching the Gospel *Trumps* Our Politics

There are numerous times when Jesus and the apostles refrained from engaging with the political process so that they could focus on gospel proclamation and disciple making.

In Luke 12, for example, Jesus was asked by the younger of two brothers to adjudicate a social justice complaint on his behalf, one particularly relevant in first-century Palestine: The older brother was using his position and existing laws to cheat the younger brother out of his rightful inheritance (v. 13). This younger brother had a legitimate social justice complaint!

Now, if we know anything about the ministry of Jesus, we know *he cared about justice.* He explicitly condemned greedy exploitation, particularly by the powerful against the weak. In Luke 16 he went so far as to say that religious people in positions of power who did not use that power to lift up others were in danger of hellfire, *regardless* of the fervency of their religion (vv. 19–31). In the parable of the good Samaritan, Jesus said his followers were *responsible* to address injustices even if they had no part in creating them (10:29–37). Note that these teachings of Jesus are on either side of the account of the brother's request in Luke 12. Jesus cared about justice!

Yet in Luke 12, instead of giving a specific—you might even say political—answer to this social justice complaint, Jesus withheld his opinion. Instead he said, "Man, who made *me* a judge or arbitrator over you?" (v. 14, emphasis mine). He then preached a sermon on greed, warning *both* brothers about the idolatry of money.

Why not give his opinion on this case? Did he not care, or did he not feel as though he had a very good answer?

The Welsh preacher Martyn Lloyd-Jones said that it wasn't because Jesus felt unqualified to give an answer. Unquestionably, his judgment would have been right! He was, after all, wiser than Solomon. And obviously it wasn't that he didn't care. Rather, Lloyd-Jones said, it was because had he weighed in on this one, two things likely would have happened: First, he would have cut off from his influence anyone in Israel who agreed with the older brother; second, the next day he likely would have had a line a mile long of people wanting him to weigh in on their justice issues, which would have kept him from his primary mission, preaching the gospel and making disciples.[14] Involving himself in this question would have taken Jesus away from his primary agenda, seeking and saving the lost. So he sat this one out so he could stay on mission.

Consider this: After Jesus had fed five thousand people by multiplying a little boy's Hebrew Happy Meal, everyone wanted to make him king, because here was a leader who could end the problem of poverty and solve world hunger. But when Jesus heard this, he withdrew—he ran away (John 6:15)—and came back preaching the gospel, arguing that the most important point of the miracle was demonstrating that he himself was the bread of life. It's not that Jesus didn't care about world hunger—he commands us to get involved in relieving that—just that the more important assignment was preaching the gospel that provided the bread of life for our souls. *When providing physical bread distracted from his emphasis on eternal bread, Jesus withdrew from the former to focus on the latter.*

Paul showed similar restraint in Romans 14. In discussing a controversy threatening to tear apart the early church, Paul dialed back his perspective, even though he strongly believed he was in the right on the issue, in order to preserve the unity of the church and advance the gospel (vv. 13–17).[15] The question he was dealing with was not overtly political, but the overarching principle behind Paul's restraint was the same. The unity of the church and the forward progress of the mission were more important than uniformity in certain things, even things Paul thought were important and about which Paul was convinced he was right.

Or consider this: The Roman Empire was *filled* with political problems, institutionalized injustices far worse than anything we currently deal with in Western countries. And yet the apostles devoted very little canonical ink to addressing any of them.

Why? It seems fairly obvious: Once the tip of the Christian spear became political reform, that would undermine, if not altogether eliminate, Christians' commission to preach the gospel and make disciples. The gospel can work in politics, but it also works before, above, and beyond politics. So for the apostles, preaching the gospel trumped political engagement. The gospel changes everything, but sometimes they dialed back their political reform so they could more effectively preach it. The gospel they preached laid the bedrock for the most needed reforms, but the apostles did not lead them.

I have a pastor friend who stumps with the Republicans and another who marches with the Democrats. Both passionately believe they march for righteousness and stand for justice. Both sincerely believe they are letting the gospel worldview work its way into their politics. Both, in my opinion, are wrong—not necessarily in regard to the particular issues they are passionate about, but wrong in letting Christ's mission become entangled with the name of a political party. Both should take a cue from what Jesus did with the feuding brothers in Luke 12.

Carl F. H. Henry said,

The clergy have neither a divine mandate nor authority nor special competence to articulate particular programs of

politico-economic action and when they pronounce their falli-
ble ideas with presumptive piety they encourage public doubt
about the church's possession of an authentic word of God in the
theological and moral realm.[16]

Or as I put it to our church, I might be wrong about global warming,
but I'm not wrong about the gospel, and I refuse to let my opinions on
the former keep people from hearing me out on the latter.

There's a time to bow out of a discussion, even when we *know*
we're right, because taking sides in a certain discussion keeps us
from the one thing we're most supposed to be doing, the one thing
that *only* we as Jesus' witnesses can do. I know for a fact that very
few lost Republicans go to the church of my pastor friend who iden-
tifies with Democrats. Most won't even visit. His is "the Democrat
church." The same is true, in reverse, with my Republican pastor
friend.

Are either fully engaging the communities God has called them
to reach?

I'm not their judge. I know deep down they want to see justice, and that's a good thing. But I do know why Jesus *said* we're
here: to testify, to be his witnesses to Republicans, Democrats, and
Independents. That trumps everything. Helping to establish or maintain a Babylonian kingdom is a secondary assignment, a result of our
witness, an adorning of it, but not the substance of it. And sometimes
it has to take a back seat to our defining assignment.

(Please note, I am directing this criticism toward these men in
their capacity as *pastors* because as pastors they officially represent
Christ's church and are supposed to embody the essence of Christ's
mission. For members of a church, whose identities are not synonymous with the church, they might feel freer to be more explicit with
their political associations. We'll discuss these distinctions more in
chapter 7, "Rules for Peculiar People Politics.")

Again, I know that this discussion raises questions about when and how to stand against injustice, when to speak up for the oppressed, when to publicly call out and rebuke the works of darkness—all things, as I've said, we're commanded to do as well. And when to, as a pastor, post a video educating your congregation on the issues and urging them to vote.

We'll press into those questions a little more in later chapters.

For now I just want you to sense—even sit in—the tension.

And most of all to reflect on the importance—the priority— that Jesus and the apostles gave to gospel proclamation and disciple making.

We Ought Not Make It Hard for Gentiles Who Are Turning to God

There's a statement made by Jesus' half-brother James in Acts 15 that I'd love to see plastered over the exists of every church in the Western world. At the time, Jewish and Gentile believers were so divided over a cultural issue that they could no longer worship together. Churches led by Gentiles were experiencing a "Jewish flight," and ones led by Jews were experiencing a "Gentile flight." So the church leaders came together to try to work something out. Their conclusion was this: *We can never disobey the direct laws of God or condone others doing so. But we shouldn't let secondary convictions or preferences get in the way of others hearing the gospel.* I love how James, the spokesperson for the counsel, explained their decision: "We should not make it difficult for the Gentiles [or Jews] who are turning to God" (Acts 15:19 NIV). He asked both Jews and Gentiles to hold their secondary convictions (the derivative convictions that flowed from their attempts to apply gospel thinking to certain areas) in ways that would not make it hard for unsaved members of the other group to find their way to God.

I wish I could plaster that phrase onto every pulpit and over the doors of every church in America: *Don't make it hard for Gentiles who are turning to God.* I wish I could make it the headline for each of our Facebook pages! *Don't make it hard for black neighbors to find God. Don't make it hard for Democrats. Don't make it hard for Republicans. Don't make it hard for white seekers, brown seekers, or Asian seekers. Don't make it hard for police officers or public-school teachers.*

We have a gospel too precious and a mission too urgent to let *anything* stand in its way. Pastors who forfeit opportunities for *that* mission to engage in some form of nation building subvert our commission. Even if we're right in what we say.

(Some of) Those Early Missionaries Got It Right

Robert Woodberry, during his PhD studies in sociology at the University of North Carolina, made a startling discovery regarding the history of Protestant missions. It was so counter to prevailing ideas that celebrated Christian sociologist Christian Smith of Notre Dame warned him that it could end his career if he published it. It was this simple observation: *In Africa, the Middle East, and parts of Asia, the early indigenous leaders who led their countries to independence graduated from Protestant mission schools and were simply applying their new understanding of humanity to political hierarchies.* Furthermore,

> areas where Protestant missionaries had a significant presence in the past are on average more economically developed today, with comparatively better health, lower infant mortality, lower corruption, greater literacy, higher educational attainment (especially for women), and more robust membership in non-governmental associations.[17]

Woodberry then concludes, rather provocatively,

> Want a blossoming democracy today? The solution is simple—if
> you have a time machine: Send a 19th-century missionary.[18]

But what is also important to note, Woodberry adds, is that
most of these missionaries didn't set out to be political activists. As
Joel Carpenter, director of the Nagel Institute for the Study of World
Christianity at Calvin University, explains:

> Few [missionaries] were in any *systemic* way social reformers. . . .
> They were first and foremost people who loved other people.
> They [cared] about other people, saw that they'd been wronged,
> and [wanted] to make it right.[19]

Make sure you catch that. The missionaries didn't come *primarily* as systemic reformers; they came *primarily* as evangelists,
witnesses, and disciple makers. As they encountered suffering,
however, they felt compelled to relieve it. More importantly, as they
taught the gospel, their converts developed their own yearnings for
justice and began to reform things on their own. Reform was the fruit
of the gospel.

In fact, many of the reforms these early Protestant missionaries got involved in were an explicit attempt to distance themselves
from *other* European colonists who had come to exploit indigenous
peoples through political programs. The message of Christianity
had become associated with the greed and exploitation of colonists, and these Protestant missionaries wanted to do all they could
to remove that association. In some ways their political activism
was an attempt to decouple their movement from political associations. They were trying to keep Christ's name "holy." According to
Christianity Today,

In India, (missionaries) fought to curtail abuses by landlords; in the West Indies and other colonies, they played key roles in building the abolition movement. Back home, their allies passed legislation that returned land to the native Xhosa people of South Africa and also protected tribes in New Zealand and Australia from being wiped out by settlers.

"One of the main stereotypes about missions is that they were closely connected to colonialism," Woodberry told *Christianity Today*. "But Protestant missionaries not funded by the state were regularly very critical of colonialism."

I think there's something today's Christians can learn from all this. When our name is associated with a political party, our hearers associate us with whatever evil that party practices. Just as the early missionaries did, we have to distance ourselves from political corruption associated with our name. Otherwise our gospel is undermined. *Thus, our loudest protests should be against abuses associated with our tribe, because the reputation of Jesus among Babylonians is paramount in our objectives.*

Why do I say that? We are Christ's witnesses, setting him apart as holy and encouraging others to do the same. If we win a political game but tarnish the name of Christ in the process, on God's scorecard it goes down as an "L."

I was once talking with a pastor who gave full-throated, unqualified public support to a presidential candidate known for his immoral lifestyle, his degrading speech about others, and his disregard for the rule of law. When I asked why he supported him, he told me it was because this particular candidate was the only one who would stand up for the rights of Christians around the world. This candidate and this candidate alone, this pastor said, had the backbone to push back against the destructive gender-confusing ideology being forced into public discourse. Plus, he said, "When you've got someone sitting across the table from the shah of Iran, I want the meanest son of a &!+#@ in America!"

My issue with this pastor was not his personal support of this candidate. I believe he was right about many of the things he said. And I realize that sometimes in politics you have to deal with the options in front of you, which means choosing whichever imperfect candidate you believe will do the most good and the least harm. What I fault him for is his *unqualified* support, for making his and his church's name synonymous with this candidate, and for hardly ever speaking out against the evils of this candidate out of fear it might hurt the candidate's chances at reelection.

Choosing between the *lesser* of two evils may indeed be necessary, but it still means choosing an *evil*, and we have to make it clear that the name of Christ is *not* associated with that evil.

In the third commandment, God charged his people never to take his name in vain, which means never to associate the splendor of his name with things that undermine his reputation in the world.[20]

Jesus' reputation is the most valuable commodity of the church; his is the only name under heaven by which we can be saved, his finished work our only hope of salvation. The way to him must be kept clear. Saddling the sacred name of Jesus to the back of a donkey or an elephant will inevitably violate the third commandment.

So let's return to our initial question: Why are we here, in Babylon . . . at the White House, having dinner with the president?

To testify to our true King.

To make clear who he is and what kind of kingdom he brings.

That trumps every other agenda.

That is why we're here.

CHAPTER 5

If You Want to Make a Difference, You Gotta Be Different

*No one ever made a difference by
being like everyone else.*
—P. T. BARNUM IN *THE GREATEST SHOWMAN*

*We are so utterly ordinary.... We are spiritual
pacifists, non-militants, conscientious objectors
in this battle-to-the-death with principalities
and powers in high places ... content to sit by
and leave the enemies of God unchallenged. The
world cannot hate us, we are too much like its
own. Oh that God would make us dangerous!*
—JIM ELLIOT[1]

I grew up weird. Not Netflix-documentary weird, but weird. In the small rural Baptist subculture I grew up in, we *prided* ourselves on living as distinctly as possible from the world. Being weird was proof of godliness.

We dressed differently. Our dress code was straight out of *Little House on the Prairie*, with a few trendy fashion flares we picked up from *The Brady Bunch*.

We didn't go to the movies. Even if you were there to see *Bambi*, someone might think you were there to see *Risky Business* and your public viewing of *Bambi* might make them stumble.

As boys we wore our hair short, even though the style for boys in the late 1970s and early '80s was long and wavy. We didn't have beards. Sure, in all the pictures in our KJV Bibles, Jesus had long hair and a beard, but those pictures were drawn by liberals, because only liberals like art.

We didn't get tattoos or wear earrings. Only gangs and the gay community did that.

We didn't dance. Dancing would make you want to fornicate.

We didn't listen to rock music, because that would make you want to dance, and we all knew where dancing led. As a sixteen-year-old, when I got serious with God, I burned all my secular music CDs and cassette tapes. There's nothing like the acrid smell of melting Journey, REO Speedwagon, and Michael Jackson mix tapes that says to a watching world, "Our God is awesome." I started listening to Southern gospel because that was "Christian" music. I avoided any so-called Christian music with a worldly rock beat, because that was mixing God's message with Satan's rhythms, "like serving a T-bone steak on a platter of manure," I was told. Apparently, God likes tight vocal harmonies and baroque cadence, and it's Satan who prefers drums, synthesizers, and electric guitars. Plus, you never knew what sneaky liberals, atheists, and Satanists had backmasked into your music.[2] And if you don't know what backmasking is, google it. You'll thank me later.

We didn't just go to church. We *lived* at church. The highest virtue was never missing a service, Sunday morning, Sunday night, or Wednesday night. Three to thrive, baby! Not to mention revivals that lasted longer than Old Testament genealogies and altar calls that could go on for thirty-five minutes without repeating a single verse from "Just as I Am." Missing church for a ball game was basically a one-way ticket to Apostasyville.

"Come out from among them, and be ye separate, saith the Lord" was the command, and we took it seriously (2 Cor. 6:17 KJV).

As I reread those last few paragraphs, maybe it was Netflix-documentary weird. But this was what we thought the command to "be ye separate" meant.

I've since come to understand that Peter had something else in mind when he told us to set apart Christ as holy. He indeed meant for us to be distinct ("peculiar," as the KJV renders it), but not primarily in the way we look, the grooming of our facial hair, or the cadence of our music. If you took a snapshot of one hundred people standing together in first-century Roman society, I'm pretty sure you wouldn't easily be able to pick out who the Christians were simply by the length of their hair or style of their togas. Sure, Christians embrace modesty in ways others often do not, but there was no official first-century Christian haircut, beard length, or sandal brand.

And yet God expected his people to be so different that Babylonians would be compelled not only to notice but also to ask *why*. God told Daniel that the wisdom by which he lived should make him shine in Babylon like a candle in a window on a cold dark winter's night (which are lyrics from one of the songs on the REO Speedwagon CD I burned!).

To make a difference, they had to be *different*.

Daniel has a lot to teach us here. By the way, did you know that Daniel was one of only three "heroes of faith" highlighted by the prophet Ezekiel as an example of flawless righteousness in an evil age?[3] There's a lot we can learn from how he conducted himself.

Prospered Through Obedience

But Daniel resolved not to defile himself with the royal food and wine, and he asked the chief official for permission not to defile himself this way. (Dan. 1:8 NIV)

Daniel's first noticeable moment of distinction came when he and his friends were instructed to eat the royal food and wine put before them in Nebuchadnezzar's palace, including foods that God had specifically forbidden Jews to eat. Daniel asked that he and his Jewish friends be allowed to eat from a different menu, which is always an annoying request for anyone feeding a group. It was especially gutsy for a prisoner to make this request. At first, Daniel's supervisor demurred, but Daniel eventually convinced him to let them try it for ten days. Daniel said,

> "[After the ten days] compare our appearance with that of the young men who eat the royal food, and treat your servants in accordance with what you see." (v. 13 NIV)

At the end of the ten days, they looked healthier and better nourished than any of the young men who ate the royal food.

> In every matter of wisdom and understanding about which the king questioned them, he found them ten times better than all the magicians and enchanters in his whole kingdom. (v. 20 NIV)

God used the distinctiveness created by their obedience to direct attention to himself by prospering Daniel and his friends. I'm not sure whether "ten times better" is literal or a figure of speech, but whatever happened, it was noticeable. God often prospers his people as they live by his principles. Their prosperity demonstrates that his ways are superior, more in harmony with the created order, and divinely blessed by the supreme Creator.

Let's call this "Method 1" of how God uses us to direct attention to himself.

Willing to Suffer

Ah, but there's another way God used their choice to live distinctly to direct attention to himself. We'll call this "Method 2." This incident took place on a gigantic plain outside Babylon.

The palace commanded everyone in Babylon to gather on a plain and bow to a golden statue that Nebuchadnezzar had erected of himself. Shadrach, Meshach, and Abednego, Daniel's three friends, refused, and Nebuchadnezzar had them thrown into a fiery furnace.[4] In that furnace God protected them, but what most stood out to Nebuchadnezzar was their willingness to suffer his wrath rather than separate themselves from God. When they emerged from the flames unharmed, one of the first things he commented on was his amazement that they would "yield up their bodies rather than serve and worship any god except their own God" (Dan. 3:28).

Something similar happened in Daniel 6. The new king, Darius, issued an order that no one could pray to any deity but him. Daniel refused to obey this decree, praying three times a day as he always had, even opening his windows wide so that everyone could see him doing it. King Darius had Daniel thrown into a lions' den for his insolence, but God protected him and not one lion touched him. Because of Daniel's refusal to yield and God's miraculous protection, King Darius came to see both the validity and the value of God's heavenly kingdom (Dan. 6:26). It wasn't just the miraculous deliverance that Darius cited as his cause for belief but *Daniel's willingness to suffer, too*!

Supernatural prosperity and protection in obedience shows God's power = Method 1.

Willingness to suffer rather than disobey God shows off God's value = Method 2.

God uses *both* methods to direct attention to himself in Babylon, and we'll look at both more closely in the chapters to come. The point here is that both methods depend on our being *different*. But different how?

At this point, it behooves us to ask: *What are the primary ways in which God expects us to be different?* After Jesus' death on the cross, he made clear that our distinction from the world wouldn't be primarily in what we would or wouldn't eat (Rom. 14:17). So what does it mean to refuse to eat from the king's table in Babylon today?

The answer to that question is, in large part, what the rest of this book is about, but I want to establish two broad categories first, in which we can expect to be wildly out of sync with Babylon, to shine like stars on a cloudless night, to stick out like three upright Hebrew teenagers in a crowd of a million kneeling Babylonians.

Difference 1: Our Beliefs Are Bananas

We need to embrace that what we believe is bizarre, especially to those not brought up in it. In a post-Christianizing generation, that's more and more people every year. If you were raised in the church, you take a lot of what you believe for granted, but to outsiders our belief system sounds, well, *bananas*. Think about it:

We believe that a God we can't see with our eyes created everything there is with just a word from his mouth. That God has no beginning or end. He has always just been there, even though we can't grasp with our minds or explain with our words how that could be.

The two naked humans he created rebelled against his command regarding a fruit tree because a talking snake tricked them into it. That one decision is what led to all the tsunamis, tornadoes, tarantulas, and trauma in the world.

Soon the thousands of descendants of those two humans became so sinful that God destroyed the whole lot of them with a flood, except for one six-hundred-year-old man and his immediate family, whom he saved by putting them on a huge boat with at least one pair of each kind of animal. And there might have been some intermarrying going on between angels and humans that produced a race of giants called the Nephilim during this time, but we're not sure.

A few hundred years later God showed up again, this time to an obscure octogenarian and his wife in Mesopotamia, from whom he promised to build a nation. For the next several hundred years, the descendants of their family were his chosen nation, even though they never amounted to anything significant on the geopolitical world stage.

Into that insignificant nation a carpenter was born to two peasants, and this carpenter was actually the God-man. During his adult life he never left Palestine, but we believe he is the King of the world forever. Roman authorities mindlessly disposed of him, but that was actually part of God's plan, because through his obscure death he was paying the sin debt for all humanity, fulfilling a promise God made to those first two naked humans and those octogenarians. After being dead for a few days, the God-man rose and flew back up into heaven, leaving a small group of uneducated blue-collar workers in charge of telling everyone about his urgent life-or-death rescue mission.

The sacrifice of this God-man is the only way people can escape eternal condemnation. And now we, his followers, regard this backwoods first-century carpenter as the Lord of our lives, submitting to his perspectives on subjects as wide ranging as money, sex, war, and gender identity.

We call him the Prince of Peace and believe he is fully in charge of everything right now, even though the world is full of chaos and war. We say he has all authority in heaven and earth, even though people disobey him every day with seeming impunity and senseless tragedy happens all around us.

We are not dismayed, however, because we know one day he'll come back riding through the skies on a white horse with a sword coming out of his mouth that will end all rebellion against him.

Don't forget the white horse—it's important. It's accompanied by some gnarly bowls of wrath.

And then we'll live happily ever after.

Kind of strange when you read it that way, isn't it? And yet I'm not exaggerating or distorting the Christian message one bit. This is what Christians have testified to consistently for more than two thousand years. I believe every word of it is true, and ironically, I think it makes the most sense out of the world.

But we have to acknowledge it's strange for someone on the outside.

For what it's worth, in a post-Christian age, the "negative" world, I don't think you're helping yourself by editing out those parts of the message the culture finds offensive. I mean, the whole belief system, when you think about it, is nuts to them. So you might as well go ahead and embrace the whole ball of crazy. If I believe that an obscure first-century Jewish carpenter is really the God-man who died for my sins and will come back one day riding on a white horse to rule the world, then submitting to his teaching about homosexuality and marriage and generosity and power and the sanctity of life is not that big of a deal.

And he doesn't give us the option to edit either. Jesus once asked a group of would-be followers: "Why do you call me 'Lord, Lord,' and not do what I tell you?" (Luke 6:46). "Lord" doesn't mean a consultant whose advice you take or leave depending on how it strikes you. "Lord" means "the authority over everything." Jesus once turned away a zealous, religious, morally upright rich young ruler because he wouldn't surrender *all* his possessions to Jesus' authority (Luke

18:18–30). Today Jesus turns away those who won't submit *all* their perspectives to him, too.

Jesus is not a salad bar from which you take the items you want and leave the rest. He's not a build-a-bear god whom you assemble at a store from god-parts you find appealing. He's not a life coach who comes to give suggestions about how to improve your life. He claimed to be the Lord, and either he is or he isn't. Lordship is one of those words that has to be total for it to have any meaning. If you are 90 percent surrendered to Jesus' lordship, you are still 100 percent in charge, because *you* get to decide which 90 percent belongs to him and which 10 percent you keep for yourself.

When I took drivers' ed in high school, my instructor had this little brake pedal on his side of the car, and if I did something he didn't like, such as roll through a stop sign or get too close to someone when following them—he could slam on the brake. He was always so dramatic about it—he'd stomp his foot on the brake and then huff real loud and glare at me. The message was clear: *You don't get the final say in this car.* I had control *most* of the time, but he could *veto* my choice anytime he wanted. That was probably wise on his part.

A lot of people attempt to follow Jesus with a brake pedal on their side of the car. But Jesus doesn't come as a spiritual adviser; he comes as Lord. As the old saying goes, "He's either Lord of all or not Lord at all." That includes all your perspectives on morality, what's important in life, or how people are saved.

Every generation is tempted to mute some part of Jesus' message. For some, it's his teachings on loving our enemies and the need to forgive those who wrong us. I served for a couple of years as a missionary to Muslims in Southeast Asia, and they struggled with this part of Jesus' message. By contrast, the college students and professors I engage with at UNC–Chapel Hill love his stuff on forgiveness but bristle at his teachings on sexuality, marriage, gender, and the sanctity of life. In each case what Jesus teaches seems *crazy* to them.

But whether I'm working with Muslims in Southeast Asia or secularists at the University of North Carolina, I tell them that there's a lot more crazy they have to get ready for. Following Jesus not only means drinking a few cups of crazy milk; it means buying the whole crazy cow.

Many Christians think they are doing God a favor by tamping down the offensive parts of the Bible—that they're helping Christians survive in Babylon by making us less odious to Nebuchadnezzar. Daniel shows us, however, that God prospers and preserves his people *only* when they submit to him *in everything*. Obedience to God may put us in the lions' den, but God can and will preserve us there.

Compromise, by contrast, leads to extinction. Had Daniel and his friends compromised what God told them to do, I'm pretty sure we never would have heard their stories. Compromise may win you a temporary reprieve before Nebuchadnezzar, but it robs you of God's power.

In Revelation 2:12–17, Jesus commended the church at Pergamum for being faithful in just about every way—they were generous to the poor and apparently had pretty good theology, too. Yet they tolerated those who taught and practiced sexual immorality. In other words, they were pretty good Christians, they just failed to hold steady on biblical standards of sexuality. Because they faltered at that one place, Jesus set himself against that church.[5]

How could we not see in this a warning for us today? If we tolerate those who teach and practice sexual immorality, Jesus sets himself against us. People sometimes say to me, "You know, if you don't soften your stance on gender, you're going to lose the next generation." Well, if I have to choose between losing the approval of a culture and the approval of Jesus, I'll stick with Jesus any day and twice on Sunday, because when Nebuchadnezzar's fires die out, Jesus will still be standing.

Two thousand years of Christian history show us that God preserves the church that is faithful to him. In the 1970s sociologist

Dean Kelley famously chronicled the decline of mainline Protestant denominations in the United States. After two hundred years of continuous growth, he noted, they had started to shrink.[6] And that trend has only increased since Kelley first pointed it out—in some cases exponentially so.

In the 1970s Kelley was wringing his hands about a paltry 30 percent of Americans who remained in mainline denominations. Today that number is down closer to 10 percent.[7] The Episcopal Church and mainline Presbyterian Church are less than half the sizes they were in 1955. From a peak membership of 3.4 million, fewer than 500,000 Episcopalians in the United States now attend church each week.[8] Other mainline denominations have followed suit.[9] In the past fifteen years, for example, the Presbyterian Church, USA, has lost half its active members, from 2.07 million in 2009 to 1.09 million in 2023.[10]

What happened? Kelley asked. Many mainline Protestants attempted to moderate Jesus' "crazy" messages to make them more palatable to modern ears, he said. They rejected Jesus' miracles and explained away Jesus' bodily resurrection because the academic community thought those things were silly or unsophisticated. And they hedged on Christianity's "archaic" views on sexuality and money.

The irony was that the more palatable mainline Protestants tried to make their message, the *less* resilient they became. These compromises didn't lead to their preservation; they led to their demise. And, of course, they stopped having kids. But that's a subject for another book.

At the time many protested Kelley's findings by saying that modern people just weren't that interested in religion anymore, and that's why these mainline denominations had shrunk. Kelley countered,

> Not all religious bodies are shrinking. While most of the mainline Protestant denominations are trying to survive what they hope will be but a temporary adversity, others are overflowing

with vitality, such as the Southern Baptist Convention, the Assemblies of God, the Churches of God, the Pentecostal and Holiness groups, the Evangelicals ... and many smaller groups.[11]

Kelley identified three things these growing Christian movements did that mainline denominations were not doing.

1. Growing Christian movements refused to confuse their message with other belief systems or say they were compatible when they weren't.
2. Growing Christian movements made demands of those admitted to the organization and did not allow leaders within it who were not fully committed to its teachings and principles.
3. Growing Christian movements did not indulge overt violations of their standards or beliefs or behaviors by their professed adherents.[12]

In other words, it was not by *accommodating* the world that the church thrived but by *being distinct from it.* The years since Kelley's research have only seen these trends increase. More recently, Tim Keller has noted:

> The overall project of mainline Protestantism has failed. It over-adapted to Western secular culture and, as such, it can't offer our society an alternative or counterpoint to what the dominant culture already offers.[13]

Those of us who've already signed on to the whole ball of crazy know that the guy coming back on the white horse is in charge of everything. He resurrected from the dead and now sits on the throne prospering, protecting, and preserving us. Obedience to him might be costly in the short run, but he always wins in the long run. For now our belief system serves, as Tim Keller says, as a "counterpoint to what the dominant culture already offers." An unpopular one at times, but one that God rewards with divine validation.

**Be assured: Persecution won't kill the church.
Compromise will.**

Difference 2: Our Guiding Values Are Upside Down

We stand apart from Babylon not just by what we believe, but also because of the values we live by. The rest of this book is devoted to exploring those values, but let's talk in big strokes here about three primary differences between the Christian approach to life and the Babylonian one. I borrow these from a fifth-century Roman African theologian-philosopher known as Augustine of Hippo.[14] Augustine said that Christians should be most distinguishable from the world around them in three primary areas:

MONEY: Babylon approaches money from the standpoint of acquisition. Get all you can, keep all you can, and spend what you have on yourself. Maybe give away a little bit of it to show you are a good person or to gain favor with the community, but money's primary purpose is self-aggrandizement.

POWER: Similarly, Babylon sees power as something to be gathered, held, and leveraged for self-benefit. Maybe share a little bit of your power so that you get good marks for diversity, inclusion, and philanthropy, but power is the currency of self-promotion.

By contrast, for the Christian exile, Augustine said, power and money are resources given by God for blessing the community and promoting the kingdom. Believers understand that both money and power are stewardships from God, given graciously for our enjoyment, yes, but also to leave a legacy of blessing and empowering others—especially those on the margins. Our bottom line is not ultimately profitability or self-promotion but the lifting up of others and the blessing of our communities.

Finally, Augustine highlighted a third area:

> SEX: Babylon approaches sex from the standpoint of *It's all about me. I write my own rules, and if it works for me, it's not wrong.* By contrast, the Christian sees God as the author of life and sees sex as a gift from him to be used for his purposes, according to his design. Sex, the believer understands, is one of God's most powerful gifts. Like fire, it has incredible power to bless as well as destroy. If someone asked me whether I wanted an open fire in my house, my response would be that it depends on where it is. Fire in the fireplace or through the burners on my gas furnace, grill, or stove is great. Fire in the sofa, however, is *no bueno.* The Christian sees sex in the same way. Sex within the context God designed is an incredible source of life and joy. Outside that rather narrow context, its great power becomes destructive.

As Tim Keller notes: "The early church was strikingly different from the culture around it in this way—the pagan society was stingy with its money and promiscuous with its body. A pagan gave nobody their money and practically gave everybody their body. And the Christians came along and gave practically nobody their body and they gave practically everybody their money."[15] In other words, while Babylonians are promiscuous with their beds and guarded with their money, Christian exiles are promiscuous with their money and guarded with their beds.

When it comes to how we handle the "big three" above, followers of Jesus *look* different. That's because we believe a completely different narrative about the world around us and shape our lives according to fundamentally different values. When we do that, we won't need a distinctive haircut or alternative music style to "come out from among them and be ye separate." We'll be as distinct from Babylon as light is from darkness, even when we're dressed in Babylonian clothes and called by Babylonian names.

The Chevette Factor

I saw these alternative values exemplified in the life of my dad. For the record, my dad has never been in vocational ministry—he worked in the textile industry his entire life. He became a Christian the year I was born, and at first he thought God might be directing him into ministry. He quickly came to see, however, that God had him right where he wanted him—serving in the C-suite of a multinational company, in a place, like Babylon, where he sometimes felt as different as day from night.

As a kid, when I'd visit him at his offices, the security guard would raise the bar allowing us access into the special parking for executives, and I noticed that every car in that lot was *nice*—BMWs, Mercedes, and the like. My dad, the ranking employee there, drove a small Chevette—the pre-Prius Prius. I'll be honest: It bothered me that Dad's car was so much less nice than everyone else's, especially when he was the ranking employee. One night at dinner I asked about it. "Isn't that embarrassing?" I asked. I'll never forget him saying, "Well, son, everybody chooses what you want to spend their money on, and that's not where we choose to spend ours. We want our biggest 'expense' every month to be investments into God's kingdom."

My mom worked part-time as a college professor, but it seemed as though she spent more time volunteering in the church and the pregnancy support center than she did at the college, even though they were always asking her to take on more classes. I remember Christmases during which we'd discuss to which ministry my parents wanted to direct my dad's year-end bonus. As I got older, I began to put it all together—my dad and mom didn't drive the cars the other executives drove or work the hours others worked because they wanted to invest in God's kingdom, not just collect toys in Babylon.

Let me be clear—there's nothing wrong with driving a nice car, and you can be crazy generous even while driving one, and sometimes your job makes you work crazy hours and there's nothing inherently wrong with that. The point is that citizens of God's kingdom approach money *differently*. Whereas Babylonians leverage money for status and pursue success at all costs, Christians give money away and sacrifice ambition on the altar of blessing others.

Whether you're looking at their possessions or their schedules, they stand out.

My dad was different, not because he wore Jesus T-shirts to work, put a Jesus fish on his car, or kept positive, encouraging Christian music on repeat in his office. He was different because he lived by different values. Where others prized ambition, he prized people. Where some delighted in money, he delighted in mercy. These values grew out of the crazy belief system he'd adopted. He was different, and that enabled him to make a difference.

Larry Taunton tells the story of spending the last couple of years of the outspoken atheist Christopher Hitchens's life traveling around with him to college campuses to do debates. Of all the arguments Taunton ever used with Hitchens, none had quite the impact on Hitchens, he said, as his family's choice to adopt a special-needs Ukrainian orphan named Sasha. *Why would you do that? Why bring those kinds of problems into your life?* Hitchens asked. Taunton explained that it was because God is a God of love, and the love he showed for us makes us want to show it to others. Hitchens concluded, *I don't believe Christianity, but something in it compels people to get involved in the worst situations on the planet.*[16]

God *wants* to honor his people by crowning them with the beauty of his presence, but he can do that only if we're different. So . . .

Get Ready to Be Weird

Like Daniel, believers in Babylon today will be tested. In lots of places and in lots of ways. The places we are tested are as unique as the situations we find ourselves in.

For you it might be reaching out to your child's teachers to see how you can bless and serve them, adopting a special-needs child, moving into a neighborhood full of refugees, or devoting part of your business's profits to invest in a marginalized community.

In everything we do we seek to demonstrate the beauty of our home country, a beauty founded on different beliefs and shaped by different values.

Expect setbacks. Sure, Daniel and his friends prospered, but they faced a lot of angry kings, fiery furnaces, and lions' dens along the way. You will, too. But God has already determined that his kingdom wins in the end, and that's good news for exiles.

God put us here to testify to that coming kingdom, and he promised us his power as we do so (Acts 1:8; Matt. 28:18–20). Right now, the "sun" of God's presence, King Jesus, has returned to heaven, and for the time being we're like the moon that reflects the sun while it's hidden from view on the other side of the earth, glowing with the assurance that in just a few hours we'll see the sun again. When we "glow" with kingdom values, we assure the world that the resurrected Jesus is returning soon.

So expect setbacks, but remember they're only temporary. King Jesus wins in the end.

He promised, after all, that not even the gates of hell would be able to prevent our forward progress. In G. K. Chesterton's classic *The Everlasting Man*, he talks about the "five deaths of the faith," five eras of Christian history, he says, when powerful forces threatened to stamp out the faith—for example, the third-century Arian challenge to the deity of Christ, or the rise of skepticism through Voltaire, or the challenge of scientism brought by Charles Darwin. Modern Nebuchadnezzars. But each time, Chesterton says, the faith emerged stronger than ever.

He then concludes with classic British understatement: "At least five times . . . the Faith has to all appearances gone to the dogs. But in each of these five cases *it was the dog that died*."[17]

Jesus stands ready to validate his kingdom in our generation, but he does so only through those willing to set themselves apart from the kingdom of Babylon.

If you want to make a difference, you have to be different.

The commitment to be different comes with its own temptation, however. And it's one that threatens to obscure the gospel almost as much as compromise does.

CHAPTER | 6

Avoiding the Culture War Detour

*Do not let your prophets ... deceive you, and do
not listen to the dreams that they dream, for it
is a lie that they are prophesying to you in my
name; I did not send them, declares the LORD.*

—JEREMIAH 29:8–9

My friend Carl finished in the top three of every high school cross-country event he ever ran, except for his first varsity meet, in which he came in dead last.

Carl hadn't been paying attention when his coach explained that in the final leg of the race the trail split and he should follow the blue arrows, not the yellow ones. During the explanation Carl had his headphones on full volume, trying to get himself psyched up. He heard nothing about multicolored arrows.

When he came to the split, Carl was at least two hundred yards ahead of everyone else, and that presented him with a dilemma. If he waited to see which way the next runner went, he'd squander his amazing lead. So he took a guess—yellow arrows it was! But instead of guiding him out of the woods into the final, victorious half kilometer of his race, the yellow arrows led him down a scenic seven-kilometer detour through the woods.

When he finally got to the finish line, he said, the stadium was empty. His bus was the only vehicle left in the parking lot. He never even broke stride, running right up to the bus and right past his coach. He never made eye contact. He sat down at the back of the bus, put on his headphones, and never brought up the event again.

Detours can ruin your race, even if you keep an excellent pace. Exiles in Daniel's day faced a handful of alluring detours, detours that would have led them miles off course from what God wanted to do in their generation. Let's take a brief look at them, because they are similar to detours we are presented with today.

Let's Go Back to Jerusalem!

Some would-be prophets in Daniel's day urged the exiled Israelites to resist any form of integration because, they said, any day now God would be returning them to their homeland (Jer. 28:1–4); he would raise up a new Moses to inflict a series of plagues on Babylon and lead the people back to their promised land.

Or perhaps he'd raise up a new David who would bring down the Babylonian Goliath from within. Hadn't God promised that by faith one Israelite soldier could put a thousand unbelieving soldiers to flight (Deut. 32:30)? "Amen and yes, please," these Israelites prayed. "Lord, raise up our David with his satchel full of faith rocks!"

Be ready, these would-be prophets proclaimed. *Live as separately from Babylon as you can, so that when God opens the door, you're ready to flee this wicked place.*

God said through Jeremiah, however, that these were false prophets.[1] Of course, God *could* have done those things, and at previous points in history he *had* done those things.

But that wasn't what he was doing now.

Today, he told them, I am doing something different.

One day God would send a new Moses who would do a lot more than deliver the people from Pharaoh and Nebuchadnezzar; he'd deliver them from death itself. And he'd raise up a truer and better David who would slay more than a nine-foot giant; he'd strike down and behead the curse of sin itself. Moses and David had been faint signposts of a much greater deliverance coming through a far superior Savior. And one day, after conquering sin and death and returning to heaven for a while, the true Savior will return to earth, establishing a kingdom in which his people will reign with him on earth, a kingdom in which every injustice will be righted, every disease healed, every tear wiped away, every Nebuchadnezzar dethroned, and the lion will lie down peacefully with the lamb.

One day.

But that day was not today, God told the Israelites.

For right now, God said, I have a different agenda.

That agenda is for you to be my witnesses, testifying to the kind of king I am and the kind of kingdom I lead. That's where my power, he said, will be available to help you. If you want to experience that power, *that's* the agenda you should pursue.

I didn't put you into Babylon to overthrow it and bring in my kingdom, God said to the exiled Israelites. I put you there to shine like stars in the Babylonian sky (Dan. 12:3). As witnesses.

But staying sequestered in holy huddles, ready to flee or revolt, and denouncing Nebuchadnezzar *felt so right* to many of them. Issuing righteous invectives felt so holy and so, well, *satisfying*. God said, however: Live among the Babylonians. Put down roots. Be friendly to them. Work for "the welfare of the city where I have sent you into exile, and pray to the LORD on its behalf, for in its welfare you will find your welfare" (Jer. 29:5–7).

Six hundred years later, on a mountaintop just outside Jerusalem, Jesus had a similar discussion with his disciples. He had resurrected from the dead, and he was about to ascend into heaven. The disciples had seen him walk on water, multiply food, pull gold from a fish's mouth, and walk through walls. Surely now, they thought, he was ready to take on Caesar. And so they asked him,

Lord, will you at this time restore the kingdom to Israel? (Acts 1:6)

Jesus responded by telling them not to concern themselves, but instead to receive the power that would come upon them to be his witnesses (vv. 7–8).

In other words, *Kingdom restoration is not what I want you to be concerned with right now.* Instead, Jesus said, *I'm giving you my power* for witness. *Go to lost Babylons all over the world and tell them about me. Let them experience my holiness, my goodness, my grace, and my love through you.*[2] Witness, not kingdom building, was the assignment.

Exiled believers today face temptations similar to those faced by the Israelites of Jeremiah's day. There's the temptation, on the one hand, to stay sequestered in our holy huddles, issuing prophetic condemnations against the culture. To live so "rapture ready" that we are disconnected from our society and its problems, thinking of society's ills as secularism's problems that we should avoid, not our problems that we should help solve. On the other hand, there's the temptation to overthrow Babylon and establish God's kingdom through political, legislative, military, or social media force, to bring in the fullness of the kingdom of God by dominating government and other power structures in society.

As we've seen (and will dive into more in the next chapter), there's a role for good politics. Jesus intends for us to work for justice and shalom and to be salt and light in whatever palaces he puts us in.

But be very clear: *Regime change* is not the tip of our missional spear. *Witness* is.

Jesus told us that when and how he returns to set up his kingdom is not to be our concern (Acts 1:7). When the disciples asked,

"Will you at this time restore the kingdom?" Jesus didn't say, "When will *I* restore my kingdom? That's what I'm leaving you here to do!" Of course not—they couldn't build the kingdom without the King! Jesus told Pilate that his kingdom was not of this world. If it was, he said, his servants would fight to bring it in.[3] Jesus' kingdom is from another world, and only he can bring it in its fullness to earth.

For now God has established his people as a faithful, beautiful, testifying community of witnesses, doing good works in government, the arts, business, and education as signs of his coming kingdom. Or, to use missionary Lesslie Newbigin's terms, in this age of exile we *provide signs*, *offer a foretaste*, and *yield ourselves to be instruments* of God's kingdom.[4]

Thus, as Tim Keller says,

> The proper cultural strategy (right now) is faithful presence within—not pulling away from the culture, and not trying to take it over. "Faithful presence within" first means being faithful; it means we're not going to assimilate, [but] we're going to be distinctively Christian. It's about an attitude of service, uncompromising in our beliefs, but not withdrawing, and not trying to dominate.[5]

There's also a time and place to be separate. To surround ourselves with Christian community that can build us up, and to surround our children with godly mentors who can shape their lives (Prov. 13:20). But God put us in Babylon primarily to live among Babylonians. To be God's witnesses to Nebuchadnezzar, we have to live in his palace and adopt his customs.

We're called neither to culture war nor to isolation, but to something radically different, "faithful presence within." Aaron Renn is correct that our new "negative world" calls for new approaches in missiology, but at its core our commission hasn't changed—it has been, and always will be, in this age, to *make disciples*. And while I can appreciate Renn's positive, neutral, and negative world distinctions, we should be careful not to overplay them. The church has *always* existed as a community in exile in the midst of Babylon. In different eras Babylon has tolerated the church to different degrees, but in no era have the kingdoms of the world embraced the true church and her mission, at least for very long. The kingdoms of this world, at least for right now, are still largely under the influence of Satan (Luke 4:6). Even in the vaunted days at the height of Christendom's power. Just ask William Tyndale, the radical Reformers, the first Baptist pioneers to America, the Great Awakening evangelists, or the early abolitionist and civil rights preachers how "positive" they felt the world was to them.

H. Richard Niebuhr's famous book *Christ and Culture*, which analyzed the different "hats" the church often feels forced to wear in regard to culture, was written in 1975 during what Renn would consider the height of the "positive" era for Christianity in America. And even now, in our "negative" world, many secularists and atheists are starting to acknowledge the positive and indispensable value that a Christian worldview has on society (think Jordan Peterson and even Richard Dawkins).[6]

Babylon's attitude toward the church evolves from era to era, but it remains largely opposed, and thus the church exists primarily as a faithful presence within a negative climate, even in the most positive of days. Therefore our central assignment remains the same: As exiles, we witness to our true and coming King.

Adopting the posture of faithful presence within changes our rules of engagement in three primary ways.

1. A Clarified Commission

As we've seen, our specific commission is *to be Jesus' witnesses*. The *ultimate* value we are solving for in every interaction is *accurate testimony of Jesus.* That means in political engagement, as I work for the common good, my first question to ask is, How does what I'm doing *make Jesus look*?

In speaking up for God's truth in the public square, am I doing so in a way that presents a Savior full of grace and truth (John 1:14)? John said that Jesus' glory was that he was full of grace and truth. Not half full of each, but full of both. In fact, John put grace before truth, which is significant in Greek because they tended to put the dominant characteristic first in lists like that. While Jesus never compromised truth (because he was full of that, too), he *led with* grace and *majored in* grace. That means what people thought about first when they thought about him was *grace*. The aroma left in their nostrils after they'd talked with him was *grace.*

It's possible, you see, to speak the truth clearly and boldly and still not be a faithful witness to Jesus.

Let me say it again for you social-media warriors in the back: *It is possible to speak the truth clearly and boldly and still not be a faithful witness to Jesus.*

In his book *Evangelism in the Early Church*, Michael Green says that God intended his church not just to clarify truth but also to *convey* it to their cultures in redemptive ways. To that end, Green says, God puts into the church both "defenders of orthodoxy" and "missionaries." Green explains the difference between these two this way:

> There is a fundamental difference between the defender of orthodoxy, who is anxious to maximize the gap between authentic Christianity and all deviations from it, and the apologist [read: missionary], who is concerned to minimize the gap between himself and his potential converts.[7]

As Green explains, both defenders of orthodoxy and missionaries are necessary for faithful Christian witness. The church must be full of grace *and* truth, and in a healthy church environment, defenders of orthodoxy and missionaries appreciate each other, work together, and never contradict, even though they start at different places and present their messages in different ways.

When I served as a missionary to Muslims in Southeast Asia, I constantly had to don both hats. Sometimes, as a defender of orthodoxy, I emphasized the distinctiveness of the gospel from Islam. At other times, as a missionary, I capitalized on a point of parallel between the gospel and Islam, showing how the gospel answered questions of Islam or fulfilled a longing it hinted at. I entered into their worldview, tried to be sympathetic with them where I could, and tried to give gospel answers to the questions embedded in their framework. Sometimes I found myself saying, "What Jesus teaches here is totally different from Islam," and other times saying, "See, the beauty and the good that you yearn for in Islam are fulfilled only in Jesus."

Paul, of course, did the same. Sometimes we see him clarifying distinctions between what the world believes and what God's Word teaches (1 Cor. 1:18–25; Rom. 12:1–2; Col. 2:8; Titus 1:10–16). Other times we see him using the former to bridge to the latter (Acts 17:22–29).

As a gospel representative, I could never fully take off either hat. But knowing which one to *face forward* in a particular conversation is crucial for effective witness. And it requires discernment from the Spirit.

Tim Keller compared the balance of these two responsibilities to the red and white blood cells in our bodies. Too many white blood cells (leukocytosis) and you'll die; the same happens if you have too many red blood cells (polycythemia). Attempting to be an entirely "red blood cell" church (evangelistic zeal) or an entirely "white blood cell" one (doctrinal fidelity) leads to failed Christian witness.[8]

The point is that we haven't fully done our job by merely telling the truth. Clarifying truth is only half our commission; embodying grace (John 1:14) while we seek to bless and prosper others (Jer. 29:7) is the other half.

Faithfully testifying to Jesus is never *less than* speaking with clarity on controversial issues, you see. *It is more.*

Upon returning to England, Lesslie Newbigin (a renowned missionary to India) argued that Christians seeking to represent Christ faithfully in the West were going to have to learn the skills of the foreign missionary. We're no longer chaplains seeking to preserve truth in a Christianized culture, he said. Increasingly, we're missionaries in a "foreign" culture seeking to present a Savior to a world that knows nothing about him. And that changes how we engage with people.

There's a practical consideration at work here, too. Which comes *first* in conversion: persuasion of the rightness of Christian morals or recognition of the lordship of Jesus?

I've seen dozens of gay men and lesbians come to faith in Christ, and not one of them ever came to faith because I first convinced them of the superiority of the traditional view of marriage. Rather, it was because they became convinced of the lordship of Jesus that they reexamined their views on sexuality. As one said to me, "If he really is the God who rose from the dead, then I figure he gets to set the rules about sexuality!"

Thus, I'm seeking to do more in my preaching than establish and defend beachheads of Christian morality. Sure, I teach the whole counsel of God, because that's part of the witness, but I want to use the lion's share of my communication bandwidth to present the fullness of Jesus' beauty. That includes his teachings on sexuality, of course, but also a lot about his love, his miracles, and his way with people. I know that as my hearers are won over to the beauty and authority of his Person, it leads to a revolution in their thinking on moral issues. I don't want to back down from *any* of God's standards of holiness—as I've said, that's not being a faithful witness. But I want to present the fullness of his Person, overflowing with grace and truth. And that shifts the em-PHA-sis I place on certain syl-LA-bles in my preaching. It also sometimes changes the tone with which I speak about these things.

Sometimes when I'm talking to an unbeliever who is really hung up on this or that Christian moral issue, I'll ask them (taking a cue from C. S. Lewis in *Mere Christianity*[9]) whether they are willing to punt that objection for a while *so we can consider the claims of Jesus.* Because, as C. S. Lewis explained, the *center* of Christianity is *not* a particular moral claim; it's the lordship of Jesus. He was not saying that Christian moral claims are irrelevant or unimportant, only that *the way we learn to embrace them* is by trusting in Jesus. Once someone embraces Jesus' lordship, they'll work their way outward to Christian moral claims. After surrendering to him, they'll be illuminated by Jesus' Spirit, the only one powerful enough to produce that change of heart. I tell them: "Wrestle with the claims of Christ first—whether he is Lord and whether he rose from the dead—and then, when you become convinced of that, work your way outward to his teachings." Engaging with people that way is not compromising or cowardly—not even Jesus presented everything at once! In the Gospels we see that he punted on some discussions because his audience wasn't ready for them yet (Mark 4:33–34; John 16:12). We're never free to ignore, downplay, or equivocate on the Bible's teachings on *anything*, but we can be wise about the order in which we talk about them.

An earnest man in our church recently admonished me to preach more frequently about cultural flashpoint issues. Our culture is at such a precarious point, he believes that I ought to use the majority of our pulpit bandwidth to "save the culture," kind of like an EMT would do if he found someone on the side of the road struggling to breathe.

I share his concerns and believe they come from a good place, but I told him: *I think you are solving for the wrong goal.* Our goal, I told him, is to bring people to Jesus, not merely to establish a beachhead in a cultural war. Yes, as salt and light in this culture, we speak with prophetic clarity about God's truth, especially those parts that are unpopular. But our *primary* commission is to bring people to faith in Jesus. We're called not to save *America* but to make disciples of *Americans*. The one we're first called to rescue is the dying *American*. As we do that, we bring cultural transformation. (Again, I know that probably raises some questions about when and how to speak out publicly about societal wickedness and injustice, like the prophets did and like we're commanded to do as well.[10] We'll get to that in the next chapter, I promise.)

2. A Shift in Strategy

Seeing our primary identity as "testifying witness" also shifts our strategy for engagement. In the spirit of Jeremiah 29:7, we want our communities to know, at their core, how committed we are to them and how much we love them. It's what we see with Daniel and Nebuchadnezzar.

Early on in my ministry I was preaching through Acts and I came to the story of Philip. Acts says that as a result of the good works he did and the message he preached, there was "great joy" in his city (Acts 8:8 CSB). I asked our congregation if they thought there was "great joy" in our city as a result of our ministry there. Acts 9 tells the story of a disciple named Tabitha, also known as Dorcas (tough nickname!), who took such good care of the poor in her community that when she died, people gathered at her bedside and wept (Acts 9:36–39). I asked our church if when we "died" (so to speak), or ceased to exist as a church, they thought anyone from the community would gather at our bedside and weep.

We felt the answer on both accounts was no. If anything, our "death" would mean one less pamphlet they would have to throw away at Easter and the city's recovery of a tax-exempt piece of property. Our ministry did not seem to be having the effect on our community that Philip and Tabitha had on theirs.

they had been in years, and those end-of-grade scores marked the beginning of a turnaround in the school's performance.

By the fourth year of our involvement, the school ranked near the top for end-of-year exams passed, and the principal was awarded Principal of the Year. In a newspaper interview that year, she said something like this: "Of course I want to thank the teachers for the hard work . . . but I have to give credit where credit is due. God gets the glory, and he worked specifically through the people of the Summit Church."[11]

Shortly thereafter, the mayor came to speak at our city's annual Martin Luther King Jr. rally. Durham is 40 percent African American, so this event is a big deal to the community. Local news televises it, and all the city and county government officials attend.

I asked the woman who extended the invitation on the mayor's behalf what exactly he wanted me to speak on. She said, "Well, anything. You'll have twenty minutes to say whatever you want, to explain why you do what you do. Just don't be controversial."

I said, "If you put me in front of a camera for twenty minutes, I'll probably just talk about Jesus."

She said, "Oh, sure . . . he's not controversial."

I said, "Uh . . . I'm not sure you and I are talking about the same guy." Actually, I did not say that. I thought it, though.

The day of the event arrived. I do enough public speaking that I rarely get nervous in front of crowds anymore, but I have to tell you that backstage before this event, I was a wreck. I mean really, really nervous. Like "Joel Osteen about to address the Gospel Coalition" kind of nervous.

The county manager sensed this and asked whether I was okay. I said, "I'm just not sure why I'm here, and I'm afraid what I say won't fit what people are looking for from this event." He said, "Let me tell you why you're here. It's because of all these ways your church is seeking to bless Durham." Another city official added, "At our city council meeting, we were discussing who should speak at this year's event, and someone brought up that everywhere our city has a need, we seem to find people from the Summit Church seeking to meet that need. We couldn't think of anyone to better embody the spirit of brotherly love we want to honor on this day than you all at the Summit Church."

When it came time for the speech, I spent several minutes acknowledging the contributions that Martin Luther King Jr. had made to our society. But then for the last fifteen minutes I explained how it was the grace of our Lord Jesus Christ that was transforming a middle-class congregation devoted to the American dream into one seeking to love and bless its city. When I was finished, the entire city council, plus the mayor and all his staff, gave our church an extended standing ovation.

As I stood on the stage that day, an idea that had been growing in our church finally crystallized in my mind: We're here to testify to truth, which often means rebuking the works of darkness,[12] but we do those things in the context of a massive love project. When our community thinks about us, what they should think about first are the love and grace we show them, and they should hear our words of warning from that context. There should be "much joy" in our cities as a result of our presence here.

God's purpose for his people is neither assimilation nor separation. If we assimilate into the city, losing our distinctiveness, we lose our ability to point Nebuchadnezzar toward heaven. Like salt divested of its saltiness, our presence no longer creates thirst. But salt that stays isolated in the saltshaker doesn't create thirst, either. We are to embrace "the city," work for its blessing, and demonstrate to it a Savior-King who is full of grace and truth, who came into the world not to condemn it but to save it.

As Robert Lewis says in his book *The Church of Irresistible Influence*, we want our communities to feel compelled to say, "We don't yet believe what those crazy Christians believe, but thank God they're here. Otherwise, we'd have to raise our taxes!"[13]

The Roman emperor Julian explained that part of his hatred for Christians sprang from the fact that Christian communities brought so much help to the poor that they shamed the Roman state for not doing the same.[14]

Toward the end of the second century, the early church theologian Tertullian said, "It is our care for the helpless, our practice of lovingkindness that brands us in the eyes of many of our opponents. 'Only look,' they say, 'how they love one another.'"[15]

Is that what they say about us?

At the end of the day, we must remember that each Babylonian is an individual. Which questions about the world are keeping her up at night? How does the gospel provide better answers to the questions she is asking than the ones she has now? She's not merely a culture warrior to be defeated but a lost soul to be won.

3. A Reordered Way of Speaking

As I noted previously, John described Jesus as full of grace *and* truth. And he led with *grace*.[16]

Of course, Jesus always told the truth with such unflinching clarity that it got him killed. And still moral outcasts of all kinds flocked to be near him, including members of Rome's government (Mark 15:39) and Israel's corrupt, cynical priestly class (John 3:1). Social outcasts invited him over for dinner. Exposed and remorseful adulteresses felt safe in his presence and couldn't wait to bring their friends to come and meet him (John 4:28–29; 8:11).

That's similar to how the conquering kings responded to Daniel during his exile. Daniel was so courageously truthful that he ended up in a lions' den, yet he was so full of love and loyalty to the king whose foolish decree put him there that the king stayed awake until the wee hours hoping against hope that Daniel would make it through the night. When Daniel assured the king the next morning that he was all right, his words conveyed intimacy and tenderness.[17] We see this same paradox with Esther, who courageously appeared before the king to call out injustice, yet was so loved by that king that he seemed genuinely delighted to honor her request.

It's not enough to *merely* speak the truth. The life-giving glory of Jesus consists of grace *and* truth. Truth without grace is damning fundamentalism; grace without truth is empty sentimentality. Truth without grace makes you a bully; grace without truth makes you a coward. Truth without grace makes you a culture-war hero for the Right; grace without truth makes you a beloved religious pundit for the mainstream Left. Both are worthless in bringing salvation, however. Worse than worthless, actually—deadly. Like sodium and chloride, truth or grace taken in isolation kills. Put them together, though, and they become gospel salt, a life-giving, flavor-enhancing preservative.

Consider for a moment how many Christians speak about sexual sins. Some (in the name of "grace") hardly ever bring them up, and if they do, they speak about them almost as though they are embarrassed about what Jesus says. This is failing to be full of truth.

John the Baptist stood before Herod and confronted him on the sinfulness of sleeping with his brother's wife, a sexual sin readily accepted within royal society back then. And in response, Herod chopped off John's head!

One can only imagine what some pastors today might say to John: *Oh, John, if you had just stuck to the hope of the gospel and held off talking about that particular sin, not only would you have kept your ministry, but you'd have kept your head! You might have even eventually won over the heart of Herod and his court! Your insistence on preaching about sexual sin forfeited your audience. You acted foolishly.*

But what was Jesus' verdict on John's prophetic rebuke? "Truly," he said, "John was the greatest prophet ever to live" (Matt. 11:11, my paraphrase). Jesus, and the preachers he approved of, were *full of truth*. They spoke out against sin.

Other pastors in our day, by contrast, thunder boldly and courageously from their pulpits against sexual sins but seldom seem to speak about them in ways reminiscent of *how* Jesus spoke about them. In the Gospels, we see Christ deal with a number of people in sexual sin, and in every encounter I know of, he spoke tenderly and intimately. He was as full of grace as he was of truth, and that's because he came into the world to save the world, not condemn it. *His mission affected what he said, when he said it, and how he said it.*

So I'll say it once more:

It's possible to speak truly and courageously about every moral issue of the day and still tell a lie about Jesus.

When you advocate for things that you believe are right, do people experience *Jesus* in you? Or do they merely experience the sledgehammer of truth? Is it possible you are speaking truly about Christian morals but presenting lies about Jesus?

Christless conservatism, you see, is as inimical to gospel witness as liberalism. Both detours will take you off the gospel road.

In the conservative Christian circles I grew up in, I was constantly warned against the dangers of liberalism. Compromise and unbelief were always crouching at our borders, I was told, threatening to rob the church of its power. If we failed to proclaim the whole counsel of God, the Spirit of God would leave us and Jesus would write *Ichabod* (Hebrew for "My glory has departed") over our doorstep. And for the record, I believe that! We must constantly stand guard against compromise and cowardice.

But unbelieving liberalism is not the only thing that wrecks gospel witness. Christless conservatism does, too. Keep in mind that Jesus' crucifixion was a *joint* project of both the unbelieving Left and fundamentalist Right. The Left hated him for his posture of authority and his command to submit; the Right hated him for his posture of mercy and his command to bless, love, and befriend our enemies. Both sides hated Jesus; both wanted him gone. Both thought they did a public service by killing him—those on the Right even supposed they did God a service by stamping out his message (John 16:2). Neither wanted Christ as King.

"Christless conservatism" in our day is a salt that has lost its saltiness, worthy only to be cast out and trodden underfoot.[18] As Marvin Olasky says, "Few apparitions are uglier and less useful than a red-faced, vein-popping, clamor-voiced defender of a religion that emphasizes loving our neighbors."[19]

Christless conservatives build big audiences, but they don't faithfully represent Jesus. Want to know how you can know that? Look around them and you won't see sinners and moral outcasts gathering around them the way they did around Jesus. Though big on diatribes, they're short on converts. And when they do make one, they're usually "twofold the child of hell" like Jesus said (Matt. 23:15). Their converts are not in love with Jesus and zealous for God's glory; they are in love with a platform and zealous for influence.

Our gospel commission reorders the way that we speak. We don't seek *only* to establish truth; we seek to save people. And that changes our way of speaking.

"Well, #$%#! This Is the Most Loving Anti-Gay Message I've Ever Heard in My Life!"

Several years ago, a lesbian couple started to attend our church. After attending for a few months, one of the two women scheduled an appointment with me. Through tears, she said,

I need some advice—I prayed with you a few months ago at the end of a service to receive Christ, and now I don't know what to do. When I started coming to this church, I was so excited about the God I was encountering each week that I invited my wife to come with me. She researched you and found out this church believes homosexuality is a sin, and she told me, "There's no way I am going to that church. If you want God in our lives, fine. Let's find a different church. A church where they accept us." So she found a liberal church in Raleigh and we started to go there.

"After attending there for a month," she continued, "I told my wife that God was not in this church. He was, however, at the Summit. So we had a choice. We could go to the Summit where God was and they didn't accept 'us,' or go to this liberal church where they accepted us but God was not. 'Do what you will, but I'm going to the church where God is.'"

She asked for baptism and began the painful process of severing her marriage.

Six months later, I got a request from her partner to meet. She told me, "After my wife was baptized, I finally worked up the courage to come and visit your church one weekend when she was out of town. When you introduced the subject matter for the morning, and it was "God's Love and Same-Sex Attraction," I couldn't believe it. . . . I thought, 'I knew it! This is all these bigots ever talk about. They are obsessed with us. I'll just listen for ten minutes and catalog all the hateful things he says so I can prove to my wife this is not the place for us.'"

(Honestly, in seven years, I've probably preached only two messages that were *entirely* on the subject of homosexuality. This woman happened to come on one of those two weeks!)

She continued, "After ten minutes, my column for 'hateful things' was blank, and I thought, 'Well, #$%#! This is the most loving anti-gay message I've ever heard in my life!'"

And so I scheduled a meeting with our mayor. I wasn't sure he would even take my call, but surprisingly he said yes. I asked him, "What are the five most broken places in our city?" Without skipping a beat, he told me (1) the homeless population, (2) care for orphans and foster kids, (3) newly released prisoners, (4) single mothers, and (5) high school dropouts. I told him I didn't have any expertise in those areas, but we would ask the Holy Spirit to show us ways we might get involved in Jesus' name.

A few weeks later God brought to our attention an underperforming public elementary school not far from our church. It was the worst-ranked school in our county and on track to be shut down within two years. Public schools in our area were generally leery of church involvement because they assumed it meant zealous, smiling Christians wearing Christian T-shirts, blaring positive, encouraging Christian music, passing out tracts, and giving away hot dogs at the annual school fair with "John 3:16" stenciled in mustard across the top.

Instead, we scrubbed floors, weeded beds, and volunteered to tutor struggling students. We provided dental clinics. We asked teachers to make us their first "go-to" when they needed supplies. At the end of the year, a non-Christian teacher from this school, who lived next to one of our pastors, told the pastor about a family in the school who had fallen on hard times and asked if there was anything we could do to help. We assisted them with temporary housing, and one of our church members, about to get married, asked his guests to redirect any wedding presents to this family.

Taking care of this family led to an invitation to take care of a few others. At the end of that year, the school's principal, Star Sampson, came to us and said, "We really need to do well on our end-of-grade exams. Could some of your people come and pray over our students while they take them?" So several Summit people wandered the halls of this school during exams praying over students and classrooms. It probably looked creepy, but it worked. Their test scores were the best

At this point she dropped her head and began to cry. She continued, "I've been attending or watching online every week since." She looked up at me and said, "I know this is all true and I want God in my life. What can I do?"

A few months later we had the privilege of seeing her profess faith in Christ and be baptized. Later she told me, "Thank you for not changing the message for me. It's always been obvious, to both my (former) partner and me, what the Bible says about this. Thank you for speaking the truth and for loving us through it."

Full of grace and truth. It's who our Savior is, and who we should be. The secret of Daniel, Esther, and others who have learned to thrive in a hostile culture is that they are full of both. The glorious combo of grace *and* truth is why Daniel shone like a star in the sky. It's how we can, too.

Honoring Christ as Lord means adopting not only his message but also his heart.

Jesus and LeftLinda

One more story. It's quick, and it's worth it.

A few years ago I got a letter from a young lady in her twenties that included a picture of her being baptized at one of our church services. I hadn't been there on the day she got baptized, and she wanted to tell me her story.

When she first came to our church, she wasn't a Christian. She didn't exactly fit the profile of "likely future Baptist." She had graduated from an elite West Coast university and moved to the Triangle to do grad work at one of our universities. She'd visited our church a few times with her friends, but she told me that the first personal interaction we'd had was over Twitter. She had said something snarky in response to a pro-life post I had put up. Normally I don't respond to snipes on Twitter, but I did to this one, and I'm not even sure why. I had no idea she went to our church—I think her Twitter handle was something like "LeftLinda." We went back and forth a couple of times, then we dropped it and I never thought about it again until this letter showed up at my office.

"I was 'LeftLinda,'" she told me, "and I didn't like your pro-life stance. But I kept coming to the church, and eventually I was convinced by the truth of the gospel." She'd been attending for several months now and growing by leaps and bounds.

She told me, "I knew you were pro-life; I knew you thought gay marriage was wrong. I knew that . . . but even with those things you didn't make the Summit the 'Republican church.' If you had, I never would have been able to bring myself to go. But because you didn't, I heard the gospel and I got saved." Now she's in the process of reexamining everything. Some of her politics are changing because her heart has changed.

The salvation of LeftLinda is the agenda of Christ's exiles in Babylon. God put us here with the explicit primary commission to seek and save *her*. Our primary objective determines our primary strategy.

Witness is the defining identity of the Christian, and "make disciples" is our central commission. Everything else we do is ultimately in service to these. It's not that any of these political issues are unimportant—just that the gospel is that much more important. As a *primary* strategy for the church, political activism is a detour.

But, like I said, that doesn't mean we should avoid it altogether.

CHAPTER | 7

Яules foя Peculiaя People Politics

Therefore I testify to you this day that I am
innocent of the blood of all, for I did not shrink
from declaring to you the whole counsel of God.

—ACTS 20:26–27

According to an old Scottish proverb, "For every one mile of road, there's two miles of ditch." When it comes to engaging in Babylonian politics, Christians in exile tend to veer into one of two possible ditches.

The first is acting as if earthly politics are the most important thing. As the old saying goes, "The first thing to say about politics is that politics are not the first thing." Jesus didn't come preaching *primarily* political change because the solutions we needed were not primarily political ones. Our problems, he said, went much deeper than any political solutions could fix. So Jesus aimed first at the heart. It is from the heart that the brokenness, corruption, greed, and defilement that corrupt our societies come (Matt. 15:19). We have multiple examples of Jesus and the apostles avoiding political entanglement so they can focus on gospel proclamation.

If the ditch on one side of the road is expecting *too much* from politics, the ditch on the other side is expecting *too little*. Good politics are a way of fulfilling the call of Jeremiah 29:7 to seek the good of the city in which we dwell as exiles. "Good politics," it has been said, "are a way of loving your neighbor." As we've seen, Jesus called his followers to be salt and light in all spheres of society, bringing his shalom, his peace, into every dimension.[1]

As we've seen, the reality is that many of the freedoms, blessings, and social virtues we most celebrate today came from *Christians who got involved* in the public square, from exiles who didn't sequester themselves in communes singing kumbaya and waiting for the rapture. By contrast, many of our greatest societal evils—things such as systematized slavery and institutionalized racism and bigotry—came from Christians *failing* to apply the Christian worldview in the public square. In his "Letter from a Birmingham Jail," for example, Martin Luther King Jr. chastised American Christians for sitting on the sidelines while injustice reigned. He wrote,

> [In the days of the early church], wherever the early Christians entered a town the power structure got disturbed. . . . But they went on with the conviction that they were a "colony of heaven" and had to obey God rather than man. They were small in number but big in commitment. They were too God-intoxicated to be "astronomically intimidated." They brought an end to such ancient evils as infanticide and gladiatorial contests.
>
> Things are different now. The contemporary Church is so often a weak, ineffectual voice with an uncertain sound. It is so often the arch-supporter of the status quo. Far from being disturbed by the presence of the Church, the power structure of the average community is consoled by the Church's silent and often vocal sanction of things as they are.

Steering between those two ditches, our goal in earthly politics is to bring blessing to our cities and, *most of all*, to testify with clarity about our true and coming King.

Toward that end, I want to offer five foundational "rules" for believers seeking to fulfill the role of faithful kingdom representatives. Honestly, I don't think any of it should really even be *controversial*. I know from experience, however, that some of it will be. That probably says more about how far we've traveled down the detour of earthly politics than it does about the lack of biblical clarity around these five rules.

I believe the following rules apply to believers in democracies everywhere, at all times, and are applicable to both the political Left and the political Right.

1. Speak Clearly Where the Bible Speaks Clearly

We must never hesitate or equivocate on something directly spelled out in Scripture. For example,

> *Abortion is the willful termination of an innocent human life. By any definition, that is murder. God will not hold guiltless those who take innocent life or those of us who sit idly by as others do.*[2] Full stop.
>
> *God created two genders. He wrote gender into our chromosomes. How we feel about our gender has no bearing on created, scientifically verifiable reality.*[3] *Rejecting this created order is rebellion of the highest order.*[4] Full stop.
>
> *Marriage is an institution God established at creation for one man and one woman.*[5] Full stop.
>
> *Racism and discrimination based on race are wrong. Humans come from a single origin; we are of one blood and we each possess the image of God. All of us have equal worth in the eyes of God and all of us are worthy of equal rights, protections, and privileges before the law.*[6] Full stop.

It is the responsibility of the strong to care for the weak, and it is the responsibility of the privileged to look out for the vulnerable.[7] Full stop.

On each of these, the Bible speaks clearly. So, again, *full stop*.

All of these are *justice* issues—that is, promoting them is a way of loving our neighbors, and staying silent on them is an act of *injustice* on our part. Denying any of them leads to human suffering. Racism oppresses. Abortion kills. Gender confusion wreaks havoc. Dissolution of the nuclear family promotes poverty.

Different ones of the above have been unpopular in different cultures and different times, but that has no bearing on how we practice them or speak about them. We are responsible to testify to the whole counsel of God. We do that even if it means we end up in a lions' den.

But as we saw in a previous chapter, speaking the truth must be done under the master assignment of being a faithful witness, which means being concerned not only with injustice in a wayward culture but also with what people think about Jesus while we rebuke that injustice. We must keep Jesus' name holy, and "not take it in vain" by allowing things unworthy of him to be associated with it. That means we'll take *extra* precautions to make sure we distance ourselves from any evil that people associate with us politically.

For example, I am the former president of the Southern Baptist Convention. Most everyone assumes, therefore, that I am a Republican, because statistically Southern Baptists vote overwhelmingly Republican. Thus, I feel especially compelled to be clear about any weaknesses, inconsistencies, or outright evils associated (whether rightly or wrongly) with the political Right, since people associate me with it, and associate Jesus with me. It's not that I think shortcomings on the political Right are worse than those on the political Left—far from it! Rather, it's that my *primary* concern in all things is that people think rightly about Jesus. His is the only name under heaven by which we can be saved, and I have to keep the path to him clear of unnecessary obstacles. I must set him apart as holy.

Maybe you're on the other side of me in regards to certain political questions. Maybe for economic reasons, or because of social justice or foreign policy concerns, or for some other reason, you lean toward the political Left, and people know that about you. If so, your voice must be the loudest in speaking out against the degradation of human life, the destructive nature of gender-redefinition narratives, and other destructive ideologies explicitly embraced by today's Democratic party platform.[8]

We can't be silent on these evils just for fear that our preferred candidates might not win, even if we regard it as the lesser of two evils. We're not only solving for a better nation; we're solving for clear testimony to Jesus. If we are associated with an evil (rightly or wrongly) and we don't speak out clearly against it, we tarnish the name of Jesus.

Our silence in the face of celebrated wickedness makes it hard for unbelieving people on the other side to really comprehend the glory of Jesus. As we've said, our vote in each election matters, but our witness to Christ's kingdom matters *more*. Christ's name *must be kept holy*.

Full stop.

When we stay quiet in the face of injustice for fear that it damages our political preferences, we show that we are more caught up in the politics of Caesar than we are the commission of heaven.

2. If You Don't Like the Other Side's Solution for Poverty or Inequality, Put Forward Your Own

Lamenting poverty, discrimination, and exploitation should not be the domain of only one side of the political aisle. We can draw a *direct* line from Scripture to our responsibility to care for the poor and to assist the vulnerable. More than two thousand verses in the Bible command us to do so. Jesus said that our advocacy on behalf of the poor demonstrates whether we truly understand the gospel.[9]

Thus, if you come from a traditional conservative perspective (as I do) and believe that "big government" strategies in dealing with poverty are ineffective—in other words, you're the kind of person who says that "the greatest argument against progressive economic policies is the conditions of cities run by progressives"—then it is incumbent on you to be vocal about the strategies you favor for empowering the poor. The two thousand verses in the Bible on poverty are not only directed at Democrats.

And I don't mean to imply by any of this that all those on the Right *don't* care about the poor. As economist Arthur Brooks has shown in *The Conservative Heart: How to Build a Fairer, Happier, and More Prosperous America*, many conservatives pursue limited-government, free-enterprise strategies *not* because they don't care about the poor but because they do.[10] My point is that while Christians might disagree on the best *strategy* for empowering the poor, we should be absolutely united on its overall importance. We should be known, as Christians, as those *most* committed to the poor.

How refreshing would it be to hear arguments in churches about which economic programs *best help the poor*? As a parent I hate it when my kids argue, but if they're arguing about who should be allowed to clean the dishes after dinner, it's considerably less annoying.

Does your church have ministries aimed at addressing poverty? If so, are you involved with them? Are you giving at a level where your church can start more of them?

If you don't like the other side's solution for poverty, put forward your own.

The same should be true concerning racial issues. If you are disturbed by some of the societal directives put forward by critical race theorists or the Black Lives Matter movement (as I am), what's your plan for empowering the marginalized? Are you known as a friend of marginalized communities? Do you speak out against discrimination where it does exist? Do you have "scars" from standing alongside marginalized people? The silence of large swaths of majority-culture evangelical Christians during the civil rights struggles of the 1950s and '60s is one of the great stains on Christian witness in the Western world, one that is proving very difficult to remove. Outsiders observing the actions, or the inaction, of Southern evangelical Christians in the 1960s were not presented a picture of a Savior who is holy.

Let it never be true again.

Full stop.

3. Be Wise to the Implications of Ideological Constructs

A lot has been made over the past few years about ideas such as critical race theory and intersectionality, theories that seek to highlight unjust social dynamics often overlooked by those in positions of privilege. Much of the evidence for unconscious bias that critical race theory presents is compelling, and many have found it helpful in identifying things such as systemic racism.

What has also become apparent, however, is that the core assumptions of critical race theory arise from a worldview founded on unbiblical and untrue convictions about human nature, justice, and the created order. These faulty assumptions have led to analysis that is skewed and prescriptions that are often more harmful than the injustices they purport to address.[11]

When we uncritically adopt an idea simply because we like some of the observations it makes, we bring harm to our neighbors even in our attempts to help them. It's a little bit like the old parable about the camel who asks if he can stick his nose inside your tent. Because you like the friendly camel's face, you say yes. But eventually he brings in the rest of his body, and soon there's no more room for you in there. Critical race theory highlights some legitimate injustices, but it is a worldview that brings with it more abuses, biases, and inequities than it corrects.

Of course, critical race theory isn't the only false ideological construct threatening to smuggle its way into Christians' political thinking. A recent poll taken in America found that more than 50 percent of professing evangelicals use the words "inspired by God" to describe our Constitution. More than two-thirds say that America has a special relationship to God and the success of the United States is part of God's plan. One president, as part of a fundraising campaign, offered a Bible for purchase that had the American flag embossed across the front cover and the Constitution and Declaration of Independence appendaged in the back as if they were all part of the same divine message.[12]

I'm thankful for America. I love our Constitution and our Bill of Rights—I agree with Tom Holland when he says that no government charter in history has been its equal and that it is founded, perhaps more than any other government document in history, on Christian principles. It's not perfect or God-breathed, but I'm exceptionally grateful for it, and I wish every country in the world would adopt a similar one. And, for the record, I love our flag. I cherish it as a symbol of freedom. Our history has been far from perfect, but I cherish the ideals that our flag represents. I even bought a pair of American-flag Crocs to wear on July 4, but I liked them so much that I now wear them all year round. My wife hates them and walks a good twenty feet behind me when I wear them in public, but they just feel so *right* to me on so many levels.

But our Bible must *never* be wrapped in an American flag, and Jesus' testimony must never be conflated with American history or his mission equated with American success. Flawed human governmental charters do not belong adjacent to the gospel of Jesus Christ. One is helpful, and the other is holy.

There is only *one* gospel that saves, and it came not out of a courthouse in Pennsylvania but from an empty tomb in Jerusalem. Our true King doesn't sit behind the Resolute desk and he doesn't stand for reelection every four years. He sits at the right hand of God and reigns forever.

My point is not to get into the weeds of critical race theory or Christian nationalism. I know these are complicated topics and there's much more to say on both of them. My point is to say that *ideas have consequences*, and as Christians we can't be content to snip away at bad fruits—we need to go after poisonous ideological roots.

As Os Guinness said, pastors must teach people how the whole system fits together and why certain worldviews lead to destruction and injustice.[13] In his colossal *The Rise and Triumph of the Modern Self*, Carl Trueman shows that questions such as whether "a woman can be trapped in a man's body" didn't come out of nowhere. *They are the inevitable fruits of a worldview that sees man, not the Creator, as the definer of reality.* These issues have to be engaged at the ideological level, not just the public policy one. By the time we're fighting over public policy, it's virtually too late. The camel is in the tent![14]

Of all people, followers of Jesus should understand this. Jesus did not come merely to suggest behavior modifications or propose changes to public policy. He came to bring a wholesale renovation of the mind and heart. His transformation starts with a revolution in *thinking*. That's where ours must start, too.

4. Don't Equate Secondary Strategies with Biblical Imperatives

When speaking in the name of Jesus, don't give dotted-line issues solid-line authority. On many issues, you can draw a direct, solid line from what the Bible says to a particular political choice. For others, you must reason and deduce your way there. You must take in demographic facts and sociological considerations and apply biblical wisdom and so forth. Of course, the goal of Christian maturity is learning to apply biblical principles in places where a biblical directive is not spelled out. So, by all means, form these secondary convictions. If you're a church leader, encourage your people to form these convictions and equip them with the tools to do so. But as you form these secondary convictions, live with the humility that your wisdom and your facts can be flawed.

Unless what you're saying has clear biblical support, refrain from attaching *God's name* or *the church's reputation* to it and allow room for disagreement such that those who oppose you aren't seen as the enemies of God. Someone might share your compassion for the poor even as they disagree with your methodology for helping them. Or they might agree with your desire to help refugees but disagree on the best policies to do so. Before we say "thus says the Lord," we must have a clear chapter-and-verse reference where the Lord says thus. Be aware when you've crossed the line from a clear biblical principle to an application of biblical wisdom.

As my friend David Platt says, "There are certain issues on which every Christian must agree [e.g., care for the poor, love of justice, desire for the common welfare] . . . even when there is no political method for resolving these issues upon which every Christian must agree."[15]

Jesus' first disciples offer us an example: When Matthew listed out the names of the disciples, he attached specifically political identities to two of them: first, to himself, and second, to Simon. Matthew was a tax collector and Simon was a Zealot. Given that no other disciples in his list got labels, we can infer that these two disciples were divided on one of the most pressing political questions of the day: what to do with Roman occupation. Zealots thought that Rome was an occupying force to be resisted; the other thought Rome was a provincial government to be cooperated with. Both brought their perspectives into Jesus' band of disciples. And I'm sure they had some pretty incendiary discussions around the campfire. I suspect Jesus probably made them room together! And I'm sure when Jesus gave out room assignments, Simon was like, "Aw, not that pink-hearted commie Matthew," and Matthew was like, "Not that MAGA-hat-wearing, knuckle-dragging Neanderthal Simon." As you'd pass by their tent late at night, you might have found them with their fingers in each other's faces going at it.

But here was the beauty: The unity they had found in Jesus superseded any differences in perspective they had on these secondary things. Their unity fulfilled Jesus' prayer in John 17, that they would be "one," even as the Father and Jesus were one. They would end up loving each other enough to die for each other.

That's what our churches should be like. And it's what they will be like when we don't equate secondary strategies with biblical imperatives.

Now, at this point, perhaps you're saying, "Wait, wait, J. D. . . . I'm confused. You keep telling us it is our responsibility to get involved at all levels of the political process, applying the Christian worldview to all areas as a way of loving our neighbors. But you're also telling us to refrain from attaching God's name to secondary political opinions and dotted-line issues, and to follow the example of Jesus by not encumbering the mission of the church in secondary political questions when our commission is to preach the gospel and make disciples. Aren't you contradicting yourself?"

Great question!

And no.

Abraham Kuyper put forward a distinction that I've found helpful here; it's the distinction between "the church as organism" and "the church as organization."[16]

- As an *organism*, according to Kuyper, members of the church ought to infiltrate every dimension of society, bringing God's wisdom and shalom into it.
- As an *organization*, the church has a limited platform as an extension of the earthly ministry of Jesus. As such, the church and its leaders must focus on proclaiming the gospel message and teaching what Jesus commanded—those direct-line principles explicitly stated in Scripture.

Church members, as part of the Christian *organism* in society, can and should bring their perceptions of God's wisdom into every sphere of society. Church leaders, by contrast, should (in general) limit their advocacy to what the Bible directly commands, since people tend to associate what institutional church leaders say with what God says. That's because we don't want to tie God's name or the church's reputation to something about which we might be wrong or to something about which sincere, Bible-believing Christians might in good conscience disagree.

Thus, as church leaders we limit our authority, and most of our bandwidth, to proclaiming what Scripture *explicitly* commands. We church leaders are to disciple people in what Scripture *directly* commands and let them learn to apply it in their respective spheres. It's the restraint Jesus and the apostles showed. We'd be wise to follow suit.

As part of an *organization*, church leaders preach righteousness, justice, compassion, and love. As part of the *organism*, church members seek to apply these concepts in the weeds of government, education, business, and other contexts. The roles are complementary, but in most cases they are distinct. It's important we keep them distinct.

You've probably noticed that I've said "in most cases" or "in general" and things like that a few times. That's because there are times when the dotted line is *so clear* it essentially is a solid line. To use an obvious example, if you're a pastor in Germany in the 1940s, it's not enough to merely say, "Anti-Semitism is wrong"; you should also say, "Membership in the Nazi Party is wrong." If you live in Greensboro, North Carolina, in the 1960s, it's not enough to say that racism is wrong. You should also say that refusing to seat black people at the Woolworth's lunch counter is wrong, too. So I'm trying to leave room open for those situations. As Dietrich Bonhoeffer said, "When a madman is tearing through the streets in a car, I can, as a pastor who happens to be on the scene, do more than merely console or bury those who have been run over. I must jump in front of the car and stop it."[17]

5. Never Morally Equivocate or Excuse

Every election season I'll hear someone say, "Oh yeah, well, our party gets abortion wrong but Republicans get poverty relief and structural racism wrong," as if (a) those things were morally equivalent and (b) the latter flaw somehow excuses the former one. Abortion is the willful stamping out of an innocent, vulnerable life with the state's blessing. There is no flaw *of any kind* that mitigates that kind of evil. In the same way, gender confusion wreaks havoc in society and leads to long-term, nearly irreparable damage.

On the other side, I'll hear someone say, "Well, yes, this candidate says this or that egregious or dehumanizing thing—but he's not as bad as the alternative." But words matter. Words create worlds, especially when they come from the mouths of leaders.

In one sense, I get it. Politics almost always involves choosing the lesser of two evils. But we must *never* equivocate about evil as we try to choose the lesser. *The lesser of two evils is still evil, and witnessing to a holy Christ means distinguishing him from evil wherever we find it, even if it's politically disadvantageous for us to do so.*

Remember: Our *ultimate* goal in any election is not to get someone elected but to present Christ faithfully. That means we must always come down on *his* side. Of everything. Clearly and unequivocally. Whether it's politically helpful or not. We're not solving for political power; we're solving for testimony.

You say, "Well, but what am I supposed to do when I have only bad alternatives?"

I know. Like I said, politics is a messy process. You inevitably end up having to choose between imperfect options, and sometimes between *really* imperfect options. Just be clear, through it all, to yourself and everybody else, where your ultimate allegiance lies and what your ultimate assignment is.

If you lean Left and all we see on your social media feeds is how bad the Republican candidate is, and nothing about the egregious wickedness of abortion or the troubling embrace of gender confusion by your party, then what choice do we have but to think you're more emotionally loyal to the Democratic party than you are to Jesus? And when you lean Right and your social media feeds are only about how bad the Democrats are but there's no lament or grief over the character of certain leaders in your party, or nothing about the plight of the poor and marginalized, or concerns over disregard for the rule of law, then how can we help assuming the same?

Like I said, whom you vote for is not as important as to whom you testify.

The Politics of Exile

These issues cause deep division in the church, and in part, I understand why. Political decisions have consequences. They affect so many things in our day-to-day lives. But these discussions, if done with respect to the above five rules, shouldn't have the power to divide us. The unity we experience in submission to our heavenly King should outweigh any secondary issues that divide us.

At the end of the day, under his banner is where we find unity. One of God's names in the Old Testament is Jehovah Nissi, and it means "The Lord is the flag under which we march." The flag waving at the top of our hearts does not boast the image of an elephant or a donkey, but a lamb. He's the one whose mission shapes our agenda, and his gospel and his mission are too urgent for us to let any secondary thing stand in our way.

Sometimes I fear that the reason these things still cause such division is because we care so little about the progress of his mission and so much about our position in Babylon. Perhaps that's because we are more discipled by political pundits than we are the Scriptures. Christians today spend about an hour each week in church and an average of four minutes every day in prayer, but several hours each day on social media. Maybe if we were less influenced by our TVs and phones and more influenced by Titus and Philemon, we wouldn't have the divisions that we have.

Let Jehovah Nissi be the banner that flies above our hearts.

Don't go down the distracting detour of culture war. It will take us miles off course.

Our testimony in Babylon begins by embracing our primary commission to be faithful witnesses. It continues, the apostles tell us, as we seek to

live quietly.

And then to

testify loudly.

They may sound like contradictions, but they're not.
The former is key to the latter.
That's where we're headed next.

PART 2

Live Quietly (the *Kalos* Life)

Aspire to live quietly, and to mind your own affairs, and to work with your hands, as we instructed you. (1 Thess. 4:11)

Keep your conduct among the Gentiles honorable [beautiful, excellent], so that when they speak against you as evildoers, they may see your good deeds and glorify God on the day of visitation. . . . Now who is there to harm you if you are zealous for what is good? . . . But in your hearts honor Christ the Lord as holy, always being prepared to make a defense to anyone who asks you for a reason for the hope that is in you; yet do it with gentleness and respect. (1 Peter 2:12; 3:13, 15)

Somebody in Nazareth lived next door to *God* for thirty years and never knew it.[1] Apparently there were a lot of aspects of Jesus' life that were neither pushy nor showy. Though he grew up in a small neighborhood in the bedroom community of Nazareth, there's no indication that anyone there (other than Mary and Joseph) understood the fullness of his identity. We have no evidence of him playing the God card during those first thirty years, no stories of him flying around Nazareth, walking across ponds, or bringing back his pets from the dead.[2]

Something tells me that if he had done those things, one of the gospel writers would have recorded it.

Nothing about Jesus' physical appearance or demeanor screamed "deity." If you opened up his shirt, you wouldn't find a gigantic *D* emblazoned on his spandex undershirt or an arc reactor glowing with divine energy.

And yet Jesus lived and worked in a way that eventually convinced those with eyes to see that he was the very Son of God, proceeding from the bosom of the Father.

Jesus lived quietly for thirty years. And then, from that foundation, that bedrock, he testified loudly.

We've arrived at the practical "How then should I live?" part of this book. We've established that God's primary purpose for us in Babylon is to witness to his holiness, his otherness, not to wage culture war or to attempt to usher in the kingdom of God politically.

The essence of the life God commands us to live is captured in Paul's admonition to "live quietly" (1 Thess. 4:11) or, to use Peter's term, "beautifully" (1 Peter 2:12). The *kalos* life. To mind our own affairs and pursue our work faithfully in ways that bring blessing and shalom to our cities; to live such remarkable lives that Babylon weeps at the thought of our departure even though we make them so mad that they want to throw us into the lions' den.

In this section I want to give you five things Daniels and Esthers can do each day to "live quietly." These are the daily to-do lists of the everyday revolutionary. You can practice these five things whether your work consists of directing strategic operations for a multinational conglomerate or helping fifth graders solve math problems.

Many Christians, in my experience, are confused by what it means to live Christianly in Babylonian workplaces, classrooms, and neighborhoods. The idea of "Christian business" makes a lot of *Christians* nervous, not to mention non-Christians! They assume it means opening up a beauty salon called "His Clips" or a coffee shop called "He Brews." Or a restaurant called "the Garden of Eat'n." Or "the Cane and Able Mobility Health Care Clinic." I'll be here all week, folks.

True story: An American Airlines pilot had just gotten back from a mission trip with his church to Costa Rica. The trip had made a huge impact on him, and as he taxied the 767 down the runway at LAX, he kept replaying images from that trip in his mind. He picked up the intercom to make his usual announcement to the passengers, when an idea suddenly crossed his mind. *Perhaps*, he thought, *this is my moment*. "Ladies and gentlemen," he began, "I want to welcome everyone aboard Flight 34 today, with direct service to JFK." He paused for a moment, glanced over at his copilot, and decided to go for it: "I know this is a little crazy, but would all of the Christians on board raise your hands?" His copilot shot him a look that said, *What are you doing?* In the cabin the passengers looked around to see if it was a joke. A few people gingerly raised their hands in the air.

He continued with something like "Everyone, look at these people with their hands raised. We've got four hours together. I'd encourage you to use this time to talk to these Christians about their faith. They can tell you everything you need to know about going to heaven when you die."

He put down the microphone, pleased with himself for taking a bold step for God. But it didn't, well, "land" quite how he had hoped. I mean, how would *you* feel if the pilot of your plane suddenly told you to "get ready to meet Jesus"? Some on the plane pulled out their phones to call their family members in a panic.

Thankfully, they arrived safely at JFK, and the passengers disembarked with a bizarre story to tell and this zealous pilot was met with a summons to see his supervisors.[3]

If you're anything like me, you admire his zeal. But you also might be thinking, *There's no way I could pull a stunt like that and keep my job.* And you're probably right.

Which is what makes the apostles' counsel to pursue our careers *quietly* so compelling.

Both Peter and Paul give us a "keep your head down and do your job" vibe. But don't they want us to *loudly* proclaim the gospel? Wasn't Peter the "stand up on a box and give a sermon in the temple square and three thousand people get saved" guy? Wasn't part of that sermon brazenly calling the Jewish leaders "wicked"? And didn't Paul once preach before an amphitheater filled with angry Ephesians?

Yes, both loudly testified to the gospel and both lost their lives for doing so. Yet both told early Christians to pursue the quiet life, because it would be the *quietness* of their everyday lives that would create opportunities for, and give credence to, their moments of loud testimony. The beauty found in their quietness of life would be so compelling that Peter anticipated it would drive Babylonians to *ask* the reason for the hope that drove them.

Here's how I would summarize the quiet, beautiful, remarkable life:

1. *Creation-fulfilling*
2. *Excellence-pursuing*
3. *Holiness-reflecting*

Part 2

4. *Redemption-displaying*
5. *Mission-advancing*

Practicing these five things may not seem to you like aggressive mission work, but in a secularized, post-Christian environment, it's where we start. Lesslie Newbigin said that for years missionaries *from* the West used a set of tools they didn't need back home, given their culturally shared language and culturally privileged position. But that was changing, Newbigin warned.[4] Western believers today, he said, were going to have to relearn foreign-missionary skills to reach their home cultures.

Mission in a "foreign" culture needs to be holistic, Newbigin said, showing how the gospel enables a life attractive on every level. And that means that the tip of our missional spear will be normal, daily interactions in the context of our secular vocations. Simply how we go about our lives will provide the first dramatic contrast with Babylon.[5]

These five qualities of daily life in Babylon are our first action steps for participating in Jesus' quiet riot, his *everyday revolution*.

CHAPTER|8

Creation-Fulfilling

The Great Commission is not the only *commission.*
—JORDAN RAYNOR, *THE SACREDNESS OF SECULAR WORK*

The Great Commission was not the *first* commission God gave to his people.

The *first* commission God gave to his people was to make the world a better place to live in—to extend the boundaries of Eden to the ends of the earth. When God placed Adam in the garden of Eden, he didn't just tell him to keep away from a few bad apples; he commissioned him to develop the garden to make it a more beautiful and habitable place to live (Gen. 2:15). That's what the Hebrew word *abad* implies (we translate it as "work"). God gave Adam a job as his co-creator.

Keep in mind this was *pre*-fall. "Work" was not a punishment inflicted by God because of Adam's sin, as if God's original plan had been for Adam and Eve to sit around all day strumming their harps and sipping on nonalcoholic piña coladas. Part of being made in God's image was *participating* in the act of creation itself through work.

God left the work of creation unfinished, you see. Do you remember the word used over and over again during creation?

"And God saw that it was *good*" (Gen. 1:10, 12, 18, 21, 25, emphasis mine).

Genesis 1:31 even upgrades it to "*very good.*"

Good is good, and *very good* is even better, but neither *good* nor *very good* is perfect. *Perfect* means "complete; cannot be improved upon." *Good* and *very good* mean that the essence is solid, but there's still room for improvement.

God put Adam and Eve into a world with gardens that needed cultivating, buildings that needed building, art that needed painting, music that needed composing, supply chains that needed organizing, and justice systems that needed formulating. In this unfinished world he intends for us to be his co-creators, his regents, in helping to shape a planet beautiful in form, realized in potential, and useful for humans.

So-called secular work is therefore part of God's original creative purpose. As Tim Keller says, God's first command to Adam wasn't to grab a harp and compose, but to grab a knife and shape.

> Work is as much a basic human need as food, beauty, rest, friendship, prayer, and sexuality; it is not simply medicine but *food* for our soul.[1]

What we do at work each day is how God continues to provide for and develop his creation. Martin Luther said that when in the Lord's Prayer we ask God to "give us this day our daily bread," he does so by means of the farmer who planted and harvested the grain, the baker who mixed and kneaded the flour into dough, and the person who prepared for us the meal.[2] And as Gene Edward Veith says, today we'd add the truck drivers who hauled the wheat to the factory, the factory workers who processed and packaged the product, the stock boys who put it on the shelf, and the lady who checked us out at the counter, not to mention the lawyers, bankers, development investors, and advertisers who keep our market economy humming. Each played an instrumental part in enabling us to eat our morning bagel; each served us through his or her vocation.[3]

As the poet Kahlil Gibran put it even more simply, "Work is love made visible."[4]

That gives a whole new significance to your job, whatever it is.

It means that so-called secular vocations are in and of themselves still God's work. God is active in our secular work ensuring that families are fed, homes are built, and justice is carried out in his world, which includes here in Babylon.

By the way, this doesn't require that you be involved in some lofty, majestic, "important" vocation. We fulfill God's purposes by providing even the smallest of conveniences and pleasures for one another. I am thankful to God for whoever invented memory-foam pillows. I'm thankful for the Amazon delivery guy who gets the batteries to me on the same day I order them. And to whomever figured out how to do facial recognition on my cell phone so I don't have to look up my password forty times a day. Steve Jobs reportedly said to John Sculley, then president of PepsiCo, in an attempt to persuade him to leave Pepsi and come to Apple, "Do you want to sell sugar water for the rest of your life, or do you want to change the world?"[5] I love my Apple products, but even "sugar water" that brings refreshment during the middle of a hot day is part of the Creator's genius at work.

Filled with the Spirit . . . *for Work*

The first time we see the phrase "filled with the Spirit," God is using it to refer to a man's *woodworking and artistry* skills:

> The LORD said to Moses, "See, I have called by name Bezalel . . . and I have filled him with the Spirit of God."

Filled with the Spirit. Why? To preach? To write worship songs? To pray in tongues? No.

"I have filled him with the Spirit of God, with ability and intelligence, with knowledge and all craftsmanship, to devise artistic designs, to work in gold, silver, and bronze, in cutting stones for setting, and in carving wood, to work in every craft." (Ex. 31:1–5)

Bezalel was filled with the Spirit of God to be ... *an interior designer*?

Yes. Just as the Spirit filled Moses to preach, write, and guide the people of God, he filled Bezalel to beautifully design interiors, ones that would even be used as a part of his tabernacle. But why, you ask, would the Spirit of God be involved in *that*?

Because God's ministry in creation is an important part of how he makes himself known in the world.

And to testify effectively in places like Babylon, it will take more than just preachers and teachers; it is going to take interior designers.

My suspicion is that long before Moses called it out, Bezalel had a sense, as he carved blocks of wood with his hands, that something divine was happening in his heart. Maybe you've felt that in your job, too. There's some part of your work, or perhaps a hobby you enjoy, that feels *divine* to you. It's not just that you're good at it—you feel *designed* for it. You sense a strange, almost supernatural power at work in you. Maybe not supernatural in the "walking on water" sense, but supernatural in the "I'm in harmony with creation right now" sense.

One of my all-time favorite movies is *Chariots of Fire* (1981). It's about a 1924 Scottish Olympic star, Eric Liddell, who was also a committed Christian. Liddell's primary calling was to be a missionary to China, and that's ultimately where he ended his life in an internment camp. At one point in the film, he explains to his sister, who can't figure out why he's wasting time running when so many people in China don't know about Jesus, "I believe God made me for a purpose [to bring the gospel to China] ... but he also made me fast. And when I run, I feel his pleasure."[6]

I love that phrase: *When I run, I feel his pleasure.* There's probably something that makes you feel like that, too. Maybe it's organizing or baking or serving or debating or building or problem-solving or negotiating or maximizing profit share. When you do it, you *feel his pleasure.* You sense, "I was *made* for this."

The truth is, *you were.* For two millennia Christians have referred to "thin" places where the separation between the mundane and divine is exceptionally narrow, places where we can sense the sacred in the ordinary. Work is just such a thin place—a liminal activity that resonates deeply with the image of God in us. Work puts us in harmony with the Creator.

Interesting sidebar: The phrase in Genesis 2:15 "to work it and keep it" is the same phrase later used to describe the priestly work of the Levites in the temple. The Hebrew word *avodah* can mean "work," "worship," or "service." At your job you should be doing all three at once.

To give us a way to earn money to support ourselves is not the *primary* reason God created jobs. Worship of God and service to others are his primary purposes. Good pay is the *byproduct* of good work. Our paychecks simply affirm that the work we are doing brings value to others. The real joy and fulfillment come from the service we provide.

And good work is an important part of our witness here.

Do It Well and Stand Before Kings

We'll get into this more in the next chapter, but Peter envisioned us doing our work so well that when people want to criticize our faith, they'll feel a twinge of hesitation because we are just so darn good at our jobs. To the Christian owner of a bakery, Jesus would say: Let your light so shine before men that they may taste your blueberry scones and glorify your Father in heaven.

The book of Proverbs says it this way:

> Do you see a man skillful in his work?
>> He will stand before kings;
>>> he will not stand before obscure men. (Prov. 22:29)

My mother loved to quote this verse to me. Here King Solomon, she always explained, envisioned a man so skilled at what he does that he is summoned to stand before kings because of it. And when he does, he can use that moment to direct attention to God.

My friend Mike is head of neurology at one of our nation's most prestigious medical universities, the top-ranked neurosurgeon in the world. Every year his university sends him to medical conferences around the world as their representative. Mike often finds himself in some of the least evangelized places on the planet, the special guest of communists, Buddhists, and Muslims. He opens every talk by explaining how his experience with the gospel affects his view of medicine. I asked him, "How is your university okay with that? They are, after all, not at all interested in world evangelization. In fact, they'd be downright opposed to it." He said, with a twinkle in his eyes, "Well, I'm the top-ranked neurosurgeon in America. I can say whatever I want." Mike does his work well and stands before kings because of it. And when he's there, he points them to King Jesus.

Or consider the story of Louise Celia Fleming, an African American doctor and missionary. Fleming was born enslaved, but after the Civil War she went to school to become a teacher and graduated at the top of her class. Shortly after graduating, she met a minister who was so impressed by her knowledge of Scripture that he encouraged her to apply to Shaw University in North Carolina, not far from where I pastor. Fleming graduated from Shaw as the class valedictorian. She used her degree to start an educational program in the Congo and became the Women's Baptist Foreign Missionary Society's first teacher there, starting a school said by some to be the finest in Africa. Her academic excellence enabled her to send scores of Congolese students to college in Jesus' name. It was her academic prowess, not just her prayer life, that made all this possible.

I could go on and on. The point is to be the best you can be at your work—whatever it is. Your work might create for you a platform to do overt mission work, as with Louise Fleming or my friend Mike, or it might just get the attention of a *king* who must know what drives you. Slogging your way through law school or grinding through a grueling internship may not *feel* godly, but it will be the very thing God uses to put you in a place where people have no choice but to listen to you. Few things adorn the gospel as much as a fervent work ethic.[7]

I opened this chapter quoting Jordan Raynor, "The Great Commission is not the only commission." We can never separate the "creation commission" and the "Great Commission," however, because the latter is the fulfillment of the former. The creation commission was to extend Eden to the ends of the earth, which includes bringing the healing power of the gospel everywhere we go. The Great Commission starts in the creation commission, and as we take the good news to the end of the earth, we extend the flourishing of creation.

Even in Babylon.

"No, Mr. Moody, I Don't Just 'Do This to Pay the Bills'"

I remember one of my Sunday school teachers telling me a story about the great nineteenth-century revivalist D. L. Moody, in which Moody supposedly entered a gigantic meeting hall where he was to speak at an evangelistic rally later that evening. The only other person in there was a janitor sweeping between the chairs. The janitor informed Moody he had become a Christian at one of Moody's previous rallies. Moody pointed at the broom and asked the man, "Is this your full-time job?" The man responded, "No, sir, Mr. Moody. I'm a full-time servant of Jesus Christ. I just do this to pay the bills."

I have no idea whether that story is true or not, but I never forgot it. It made me zealous for evangelism, but it also distorted my view of secular work, making me think of secular jobs as second class in God's kingdom, a kind of means to an end for funding *real* kingdom work. Real kingdom work, I assumed, happens from pulpits, choir lofts, and writers' desks. For any *true* Christian, his or her life's passion is *church work*.

While I appreciate the evangelistic spirit behind the story, and to be clear, the Great Commission and the work of the church ought to be at the center of every Christian's heart, being a full-time servant of Jesus Christ is not something we do *after* we pay the bills; it's what we do *as* we pay the bills. Cleaning up a room for others to meet in, whether that's so they can participate in an evangelistic sermon, enjoy a music concert, or take part in a job fair, is a way of serving God by fulfilling the creation commission. We may not have the chance to tell people in every interaction that the *way* we do our work and the spirit we carry with us in it point people to our Creator.

There's a quote attributed to Martin Luther that he most certainly did not say, but it still accurately reflects the Protestant Reformers' (and Peter's and Paul's!) attitude toward secular work:

> The maid who sweeps her kitchen is doing the will of God just as much as the monk who prays—not because she may sing a Christian hymn as she sweeps but because God loves clean floors.

This kind of work is an important component of our witness in Babylon. Businesses, hobbies, and personal passion projects that fulfill the creation mandate give others a glimpse of creation as God intended it, the way it will be one day in the future kingdom. Through our work, our hobbies, and even how we keep our homes, we "sketch out in pencil what one day God will paint with indelible ink."[8]

That is partially what C. S. Lewis was referring to when he described the Pevensie children's final entry into heaven:

> And now at last they were beginning Chapter One of the Great Story which no one on earth has read: which goes on forever: in which every chapter is better than the one before.[9]

God created us for work. It's part of how we worship him and how we quietly put him on display. It sets the stage for our witness in Babylon.

Excellence (*kalos*) in our jobs validates, and creates a hunger for, our witness in Babylon. Even the great evangelist Billy Graham agreed. Shortly before he died, Graham said he was convinced the next Great Awakening would happen not in the stadiums but in the marketplace.[10]

Tim Keller notes it's likely that when all is said and done, we might see that our work in the arts, business, and educational institutions had an even greater shaping effect on hearts and minds in Babylon than our legislative attempts did. That's not to say legislative action is *un*important, but, as Keller notes, as consensus was lost in the cultural upheavals of the 1960s, the liberal Left turned to pop culture, academic institutions, the arts, and the media to shape the contemporary mind, while the religious Right turned in large part toward politics. Keller asks: Sixty years later, who appears to have chosen the more effective strategy?[11]

What we do, and how we do it, is a crucial part of making God known in Babylon.

The creation commission is the foundation of the Great Commission.

CHAPTER | 9

Excellence-Pursuing

Then this Daniel became distinguished above
all the other high officials and satraps, because
an excellent spirit was in him. And the king
planned to set him over the whole kingdom.
—DANIEL 6:3

A businessman in our community told me recently that he doesn't like partnering with other Christian businesses because the ones he's worked with didn't honor deadlines or meet agreed-upon budgets and expected him to excuse their sloppy work because of "grace." He told me, "I've learned when they put a Bible verse in their logo or a Christian fish under their name, watch out."

An unfair generalization, to be sure. But few things, practically speaking, damage the reputation of Christ in our community like a poor work ethic.

According to the apostles, it's not just *what* work we do but *how* we do it that directs our community's attention to the worthiness of God. *Christ's own reputation* is on the line in the work that we do.

In this chapter and the next, I want to consider two qualities that "quiet life" work must possess to have gospel impact, whether that work is done in the boardroom, the classroom, or the kitchen.

Our Excellent Adventure

One of the most iconic movies of the late 1980s was *Bill and Ted's Excellent Adventure*. This epic ninety-minute masterpiece introduced two little-known actors to the world, a young Keanu Reeves and his costar, Alex Winter. Reeves and Winter play two goofballs who travel through time via a magic phone booth, play the air guitar, and live by the maxim "Be excellent to each other."

I'm not sure whether watching *Bill and Ted's Excellent Adventure* changed anyone's life. Sociologists, in fact, claim the movie helped inspire the slacker culture of the 1990s, the opposite of excellence. The movie was spontaneously conceived in an improv class and the script was pecked out on an old-school typewriter in less than four days.[1]

Still, Bill and Ted might have been onto something. More than 2,500 years ago, this maxim was one of the secrets of Daniel's success, too. Everything Daniel did was *excellent*:

> Then this Daniel became distinguished above all the other high officials and satraps, because an excellent spirit was in him. And the king planned to set him over the whole kingdom. (Dan. 6:3)

> And in every matter of wisdom and understanding about which the king inquired of them, he found them ten times better than all the magicians and enchanters that were in all his kingdom. (1:20)

Daniel 6:4 says that Daniel's enemies "could find no corruption in him, because he was trustworthy and neither corrupt nor negligent" (NIV). Not only was Daniel free of corruption, but he also never cut corners. He did his stuff right the first time and turned it in on time.

"Excellent" in Daniel 6:3 is our best translation of an interesting Aramaic word, *yattir*. It means "unsurpassed" or "incomparable."[2] The fire that Nebuchadnezzar created in the furnace after heating it seven times hotter than usual was described as *yattir*. It was "exceedingly" (*yattir*) hot. The idol King Nebby erected to himself was "exceedingly" (*yattir*) spectacular, and the apocalyptic beasts in Daniel's visions were *yattir* strong (7:7) and *yattir* scary (7:19), and when I was a kid, they used to give me *yattir* bad dreams.

One scholar told me *yattir* means what a little kid means when he says something is the "bestest" or "mostest." Daniel's spirit at work was the mostest awesomest of everybody's. His spirit compared to their spirits the way Nebuchadnezzar's fiery furnace compared to a common campfire.

Is that what people say about the quality of your work? Your studies? And your attitude while doing it? Are you *yattir*?

The book of Daniel makes clear that the excellence of Daniel's work and spirit was a reflection of the God he served. It was not primarily an attempt to prove himself, best everyone, get into the right school, or make more money; it was an attempt to display the excellence of God.

That's a crucial distinction. Excellence is not self-promotion. It's *testimony*.

I'm pretty confident that no wobbly chairs came out of Jesus' carpenter shop in Nazareth. As the perfect reflection of his Father, Jesus definitely would have received five stars on Angie's List. (By the way, I've always thought Jesus' furniture business could have been called Restoration Heartware.) Our goal in our work is to reflect that excellence.

Do Everything *in the Name of the Lord Jesus*

Paul told us that we should do our work in Jesus' name:

> And whatever you do, in word or deed, do everything in the name
> of the Lord Jesus, giving thanks to God the Father through him.
> (Col. 3:17)

Doing something "in the name of the Lord Jesus" means doing it as an *offering* to him. We are putting his name on our work, which means that his glory gets associated with the quality of our work. When our work is associated with his name and it is sloppy and shoddy, we break the third commandment by taking his name in vain.

Paul went on in the Colossians passage to say that the quality of our work should not be dependent on who notices or what kind of earthly reward we receive (Col. 3:22–24), because God *always* sees it. Paul's admonition is especially poignant when you consider that Paul directed these instructions to "slaves," who have the worst work conditions imaginable. Many reading Paul's letters likely would have been something closer to what we now call indentured servants, but still, even indentured servanthood was not an ideal working environment. An indentured servant had typically sold himself to someone as a last-ditch effort to pay off a debt. Since there weren't any labor protection laws in those days, especially for people severely in debt, servants typically worked in significantly unfavorable job conditions. (Sometimes we complain, "Man, my boss really owns me." For these people, their bosses really did!)

Yet even in that kind of work situation, Paul told Christians to do their work *excellently*, because they were doing it first and foremost for Christ. *Christ's* name was on the line in their work, and the reputation of his name was more important than their salaries.

Remember, the reputation of his name is *why* he has us in Babylon.

Let's be honest—it is demoralizing to work for someone who doesn't give us credit for what we've done. It's even worse to work for one who only responds with critical feedback. A bad boss can make otherwise satisfying work an absolute drudgery! "What is the point of working hard?" we think. "She never notices my work anyway, and even if she does, she rarely gives me the credit for it."

If you're working only for Nebuchadnezzar, that's a reasonable response. But if you're working for King Jesus, it's not. Paul went on:

Whatever you do, work heartily, as for the Lord and not for men, knowing that from the Lord you will receive the inheritance as your reward. You are serving the Lord [Boss] Christ. For the wrongdoer [perhaps you could read that as "slacker"] will be paid back for the wrong he has done, and there is no partiality. (Col. 3:23–25)

In other words, every job I do, every assignment I complete, every chore I tackle, every paper I turn in, I do it first for the *Supreme Boss*, Christ.

Do you really want to get the world's attention? Do a *great* job for an earthly boss who is a jerk and doesn't give you the first word of recognition. Lots of Babylonians work hard, but they do it primarily for money, promotion, and praise. Working hard for those reasons is not all that remarkable. It's basically just wisely calculated self-interest. Paul said it's when you work hard *without* those motivations that people will be moved to ask, "What in the world could possibly be driving you?"

To which you reply, "Actually, nothing in this world drives me. My Boss waiting in another world does."

Business consultants make millions figuring out how to motivate people to work hard, and usually they tap into some kind of self-interest: The thrill of winning. Praise. Money. A lasting legacy. Self-actualization. These motivations have their place. But for the Christian a couple of motivations trump them all—King Jesus' personal delight in our work and his reputation in the world.

I remember hearing one of my professors point out that explorers to the New World had discovered valleys filled with species of beautiful flowers that, to their knowledge, no human eye had ever seen before. For whom had God created all that beauty then, my professor asked, if for thousands of years no human eye had beheld it? His answer was that God does some things for his own pleasure. God sees excellence even when no one else does.

Excellence in our work when no earthly audience is watching alerts observers to the reality of a heavenly audience. It communicates in ways that our words cannot. We may say with our mouths that "Jesus is Lord," but when we don't turn in assignments on time or respect our bosses, our actions cry out, "Comfort and self-interest are my lords."

Blameless in Babylon

This aspect of our witness becomes all the more important as the world becomes more "negative." The apostles say we should do our work so excellently that, as was the case with Daniel, our opponents can't find anything to criticize us for, no matter how hard they try!

When I was in college, a group of friends and I started a Bible study that turned into a small campus movement. Before it was all said and done, several hundred students were involved, and it was bigger than anything else happening on campus at the time. Scores and scores of students had professed faith in Christ. It ended abruptly when the university president shut it down, forbidding me, personally, from teaching the Bible on campus again—because he didn't like what we were teaching, particularly the exclusivity of Christ alone for salvation and the authority of the Bible.

One of the faculty who was sympathetic toward us told me something later that was particularly encouraging. The president had lamented to this faculty member in a cabinet meeting, "Why does it seem that so many of our best students are a part of this movement?" Several of us who were part of the leadership in this group were "president's list" students, officers in school clubs, and active in campus life. A couple of us were ranked at the top of our academic programs, and a few of us had won intercollegiate awards on behalf of our school.

I'd do many things differently if I could go back through my college years, but one thing I don't regret is a single ounce of effort I put into trying to be an excellent student and excellent campus-community member.

Excellent work sets us up to talk about the excellence of Jesus.

Put Your Job in the Offering Bucket

In saying we are to give thanks to God through our work (Col. 3:17), Paul is recasting our work in the language of "worship." Our work, he says, ought to be like a thanksgiving offering of praise. That hearkens back to what we saw in the previous chapter about how the Hebrew word God used to describe Adam's work in the garden, *abad*, means both work *and* worship!

Would you be embarrassed to lay down your work at God's feet as *an offering*?

One of my friends who works as a wedding photographer complained to me that when he does contract work for other Christian-owned businesses, they expect him to give them a "ministry discount." If we do something in Jesus' name, as Paul commands, however, it should be done in a way that extends generosity, not expects it. Don't ask for discounts because you are a Christian—*offer them*! I remember doing a job one time for a Christian employer who paid me very generously. It was *so* generous I asked him why. He smiled and said simply, "Well, we serve a generous God." His generosity directed my attention to Jesus'. In that moment I loved and worshiped Jesus more because of how this man had treated me.

We pursue excellence in work because *that's what Christ is worthy of.* Excellence is not primarily about making money, bringing customers back, making ourselves feel good, or garnishing our name in the community. Excellence *may* bring these things, too, and that's fine, but our core motivator is Christ's glory. And when the other motivations fail, that one remains.

When others see our good work, Jesus said, they'll glorify our Father in heaven (Matt. 5:16).

In the memorable words of Martin Luther King Jr.,

> Whatever your life's work is, do it well.... If it falls your lot to be a street sweeper, sweep streets like Michelangelo painted pictures, like Shakespeare wrote poetry, like Beethoven composed music; sweep streets so well that all the host of Heaven and earth will have to pause and say, "Here lived a great street sweeper, who swept his job well."[3]

What Nehemiah Never Knew

One of my favorite exhibits in the British Museum is the display containing the cup that the Persian king Artaxerxes supposedly used in the sixth century BC. There's nothing particularly amazing about the cup itself; it was just the thought that I was looking at the very cup the Bible writer Nehemiah once held in his hands!

Nehemiah, a Jew exiled in Persia, had the inglorious job of sampling the wine before the king drank it to ensure it was free of poison. There had to be a lot of days Nehemiah woke up wondering what had become of his life. Here he was, a man with obvious leadership potential, serving as an exile in Persia, drinking wine to help ensure a corrupt, oppressive pagan king didn't get assassinated by one of his rivals. "What difference does this make?" he asked. "How is this a good use of my skill? Why does any of it matter?" My tour guide at the British Museum, Ben, said that Nehemiah surely had to have felt as though he was in the wrong place at the wrong time doing an insignificant job that made no difference in God's kingdom.

And yet, one day, because of Nehemiah's faithful, humble, joyful, and excellent service to King Artaxerxes, God opened up a door for him to lead in rebuilding of the walls of Jerusalem (Neh. 2:1–8), walls that Jesus himself would teach within one day, walls that the Spirit of God would blow through like a rushing wind when he filled the first Christians at Pentecost. The excellence of Nehemiah's service is what led to the moment of opportunity.

Nehemiah thought he went to work every day merely to prosper a pagan king. He had no idea with each sip he was laying the foundation for a city Jesus would inhabit.

I'm quite sure Nehemiah had no idea the significance that his ordinary acts of obedience would have.

I'm quite sure you and I don't, either.

CHAPTER 10

Holiness-Яeflecting

At this, the administrators and the satraps tried
to find grounds for charges against Daniel in his
conduct . . . but they were unable to do so. They
could find no corruption in him, because he was
trustworthy and neither corrupt nor negligent.
—DANIEL 6:4 NIV

I have a friend who built skyscrapers in Chicago. He said it was customary for the big players in the industry to withhold the last payment to contractors as a way of manipulating them into taking new jobs with them at discounted rates. It's unfair, but these central players are so big that contractors have no choice but to go along. My friend (who represented one of these big players) said that for him, as a Christian, this practice presented a dilemma. Paying fairly *disadvantaged* him, at least in the short run, because it forfeited his leverage with contractors. And yet, he said, it didn't feel right to unfairly withhold payment if the name of the Lord Jesus was attached to his work.

Our conduct in Babylon should not only be excellent—it should make plain that we serve a God of justice and fairness. Our work, if done in his name, should reflect both his excellence and his holiness. Paul went on to say,

> Masters, treat your bondservants justly and fairly, knowing that
> you also have a Master in heaven. (Col. 4:1)

Paul reminds us that in every interaction we have a Master in heaven to whom we report. If we treat someone unfairly, we can rest assured that there is a God who will do something about it even if the person we wronged cannot. He's our first Boss.

It always baffles me how certain churchgoers maintain faithful church attendance and tithe regularly while cheating on their taxes. Our God is not just the God of church on Sunday; he's God of the whole creation every second of every week.

Proverbs says,

> A false balance is an *abomination* to the LORD,
>> but a just weight is his delight. (Prov. 11:1,
>>> emphasis mine)

"Abomination" is a varsity-level word in the Old Testament. Think sexual perversion, betrayal, murder, or exploitation of the poor. The writer of Proverbs, however, says that cheating or shorting a customer goes in the same category in God's eyes. *It is an abomination* to God to do shabby work that doesn't give our employers their money's worth, our employees what they are due, our shareholders what they deserve, our professors what they require, or our neighbors what they are entitled to.

Just as with excellence, this is about more than just being recognized as dependable or getting promoted; it's about giving a proper reflection of God. Daniel 6:4 says that Daniel's enemies "could find no corruption in him, because he was trustworthy and neither corrupt nor negligent" (NIV). Daniel's work demonstrated that his God was a God of integrity and fairness.

Justice is the very *foundation* of God's throne (Ps. 89:14). His reputation for justice is also *foundational* to the world's understanding of the gospel. Shining in Babylon means never sullying his name through association with a false balance, a fudged return, or a willingness to compromise for a financial advantage.

"Holiness-reflecting" also means that the products we create and the environments in which we serve them reflect the beautiful, gracious nature of our heavenly Father. Customer service is about more than creating returning patrons, it's about giving Babylonians a glimpse of the hospitality of the heavenly Father. How we treat people should reflect the God who *delights* in serving his creatures! It truly is *his pleasure* to serve his creation.

I know of one Christian owner of an insurance company who refuses to use "derivatives," a speculation scheme that maximizes profit but exposes the insured to great financial risks in the case of a catastrophe or natural disaster.[1] Though supposedly common in the industry, and quite lucrative, this owner felt it violated the interests of his customers and did not reflect the nature of his heavenly Father.

Which is more Christian—to use a Bible verse in the footer of your letterhead or to put the interests of your customers above personal profit?

To Save Souls *and* Make Life Better for People

A small but informal group of English Christians in the 1700s demonstrated what happens when you accompany excellence-pursuing, holiness-reflecting work with Christian testimony in Babylon. Organized at Holy Trinity Church on Clapham Common in London, this group was known as the Clapham Sect.

The late 1700s were a spiritually dark time in England. Politically, things were a mess. England's resources were stretched thin trying to manage a burgeoning (and largely unjust) colonial empire, and they actively participated in the global slave trade.

The Clapham Sect included clergy members such as Charles Simeon and former slave trader John Newton (author of the hymn "Amazing Grace"); politicians like Granville Sharp; business leaders such as John Thornton; social activists such as Zachary Macaulay; and poets and playwrights such as Hannah More. Their desire was to see Christ's name magnified and society transformed in his name—specifically the abolition of the slave trade and the reformation of the nation's morals.

William Wilberforce, a member of Parliament, was probably the most prominent fellow in the group. On becoming a Christian, Wilberforce had considered resigning from Parliament so he could go into pulpit ministry. John Newton, his pastor, encouraged him *not* to do so. As amazing as he would be in the pulpit, Newton said, God had placed him into government for a reason.

Here's how Stephen Tomkins describes the impact of this eighteenth-century fellowship of believers:

> There was, in the late eighteenth and early nineteenth centuries, a network of friends and families in England, with William Wilberforce as its center of gravity, powerfully bound together by shared moral and spiritual values, by religious mission and social activism, by love for each other, and by marriage. Their greatest and most celebrated achievement was the abolition of the slave trade and then slavery itself throughout the British Empire and beyond. They were founders of the British colony of Sierra Leone, of schools, and of Christian missions, some of which continue today.
>
> A number were MPs [Members of Parliament] and used their influence in Parliament to promote causes from prison reform to the protection of Sunday, and from peace to censorship. They privately gave away extraordinary amounts of money to people in

need. Their campaigns were driven by two irreducibly separate religious motives: one, to promote true religion and save souls; the other, to make life better for people and to make the world a better place.

Neither was merely the means to the other; both were essential; both were, as they understood it, the work of God.[2]

Ultimately, historians say, the Clapham Sect helped spawn both the abolition of the slave trade and the continued religious awakenings of the English-speaking world in the 1800s.

I think what arrests me most about Tomkins's description is the group's *two* goals, neither one *merely* being the means to the other. They wanted to save souls *and* make life better by applying holiness to all layers of society. This is Jeremiah 29:7 existence. It is pursuing secular work that seeks to bless others through its excellence, honesty, and justice consciousness.

I have to imagine that Daniel, somewhere up in heaven while all this was going down, was nodding his head vigorously, because that's how he saw his assignment in Babylon, too. Everything Daniel did he did excellently, in ways that put the beauty, holiness, and justice of God on display. When Daniel pleaded with Nebuchadnezzar on behalf of justice and compassion for the poor (Dan. 4:27), Nebuchadnezzar listened to him, in part, because of the quality of his work, which was a reflection of God's beautiful character.

The Price of Compromise

Sadly, also embedded within the Clapham Sect is an example of what happens when we lapse in this commitment to integrity.

George Whitefield, a good friend to many members of the Clapham Sect and whose preaching helped spawn it, became the greatest preacher of his generation. His preaching, even more, historians say, than Jonathan Edwards's or John Wesley's, was behind the success of the religious awakenings of the eighteenth century. Whitefield's theology was orthodox. His journals, which recount his struggles for purity of heart before God, are deeply moving. I've studied them extensively— Whitefield's earnest pursuit of God and his example in ministry had a big impact on me in my early years of ministry. In seminary I read dozens of his sermons and at least three biographies about him.

But tragically, in his later years, George Whitefield compromised on slavery. He started out preaching against it. That made him less popular in some places, particularly in the American South. Over time antislavery rhetoric began to drop out of his sermons, as Whitefield seems to have accepted slavery as part of the established social order. Plus, preaching against it would have reduced the size of his crowds. Tragically, Whitefield even began to employ slave labor in his own economic projects, saying it was necessary to thrive in that economy. But, I'm sure he reasoned, overall he was doing good for society. Eventually, and bewilderingly, George Whitefield went on record defending the institution of slavery.

I still find myself wanting to quote George Whitefield in sermons or wanting to share some profound insight I've learned from his life. But usually I don't—or at least, when I do, I keep his name out of it. That's tragic, because there's so much I'd love our church to learn from George Whitefield. But, you see, there's an African American woman on our church staff from southern Georgia whose family traces their lineage directly back to George Whitefield's plantations. Her ancestors remained enslaved, in part, because Whitefield compromised, and it doesn't feel right for me to publicly celebrate a man whose compromises hurt the family of someone I now consider to be my own family.

We don't know all the reasons behind Whitefield's moral slide. At first it appears to have been a pragmatic calculation on his part—staying silent would cause more people to come to hear him preach. At some point, however, his conviction shifted from pragmatic calculation to acquiescence. From there it became a matter of personal self-interest, and somewhere along the way, that led to a wholesale conviction change.

Perhaps Whitefield's compromise did indeed lead to larger audiences for his preaching. But now, seeing the long-term damage to the gospel's reputation (not to mention people's lives), there's no way we can say, from this vantage point, that his compromise was worth it.

Don't be like George Whitefield. Though the places we will be pressured to compromise won't be the same as they were for him, many challenges remain for us. We still live in a Babylonian system that prioritizes profit and power above everything, and if compromising or bending rules is required to achieve those things, we will be pressured to do just that. We'll be told that our shareholders are depending on us to maximize returns, and this is just how the world works now. Withhold the last payment. Use the derivative. Employ slave labor.

It's easy, in such an environment, to subtly shift our convictions to go with the flow. Those subtle shifts may indeed help us succeed in the short run. We might even justify our silence, or our compromises, by rationalizing that we'll have greater gospel impact if we don't speak out against these things.

Don't buy it. Don't make some future Christian generation have to leave your name out when they tell your stories because of how you tarnished the name of Christ.

As Marvin Olasky says, "When people want us to go with the flow, to meet 'halfway,' we need [instead] to stand our ground whenever it is good ground, high ground, God's ground."[3]

This is what Paul and Peter were trying to tell a group of powerless Christian workers who felt trapped in a Babylonian system of employment. We don't do our work first for our earthly masters, or bosses, or customer base, or the shareholders, or even ourselves, they said—we do our work as an offering *to the Lord*. In all that we do, we seek to save souls and make life better. That's holiness in action.

God put us in Babylon to make a difference, and we can't make a difference unless we are different. That difference might be first and most perceived through our excellence and integrity. Those beauties pave the way for our witness. When I was growing up, my church had a wall of gospel tracts we could distribute to people around town: the "tract rack." One Sunday evening my eye was drawn to a tract poking out of the rack that looked like a $100 bill. When I pulled it out, however, thinking I'd gotten lucky, I was disappointed to find that on the other side was the message "Here's the real tip. Find Jesus."

Now, to be clear: I agree that finding Jesus is worth more than all the tip money in the world, but unless this tract was accompanied by a real $100 bill, it is unlikely to cause the recipient to start thinking of the gospel that way. The best way to tell someone about Jesus is to make their life better as you do so! And the way you do that is by giving a proper tip, even a generous one, to the waiter serving you. I always tell our church that if you're going to leave a gospel tract or a Summit Church invite card for your waiter, accompany it with a 25 percent tip. You're much more likely to give them a feel of who Jesus *really* is that way. He's a God of love, grace, and generosity. Everything about us, including how we tip, should demonstrate that.

CHAPTER 11

Яedemption-Displaying

Your faithful followers will . . .
speak of the glory of your kingdom;
they will give examples of your power.
—PSALM 145:10–11 NLT

Few things demonstrate the distinction between the kingdoms of Babylon and the kingdom of Christ quite so poignantly as *grace*. The Nebuchadnezzars of the world are usually big on taxation, self-promotion, and double standards. Our King took upon himself the form of a servant so that he could redeem his subjects who had betrayed and deserted him. Thus, it shouldn't be surprising that a sovereign God arranges circumstances in which we are wronged and disadvantaged so that we can display his kind of grace.

A couple of years ago I went through the toughest time of my twenty-five years in the pastorate. It seemed as if every part of my life was on fire—I felt hurt by friends and colleagues, unfairly maligned in public, and even misunderstood by some of my family members. I kept asking God, "Why? What am I doing wrong?"

In response God led me to a verse in Peter's letter to Christian exiles. Regarding suffering, Peter said:

For you were called to this, because Christ also suffered for you,
leaving you an example, that you should follow *in his steps*.
(1 Peter 2:21 CSB, emphasis mine)

You were called to this. Just as Jesus did nothing wrong and still
suffered, so I was called to suffer, too. I'm called to be in this generation, in the court of my Nebuchadnezzars, what Jesus was in his
generation, before his Nebuchadnezzar, Pontius Pilate, because grace
demonstrates the heart of the Father in ways that few other things can.

The phrase "in his steps" takes me back to a book I read in college that used the apostle Peter's words for its title. *In His Steps*, by
Charles Sheldon, tells the fictional story of a nineteenth-century pastor, Henry Maxwell, serving in a community of privilege, when he
is confronted one day on the sidewalk by a man in need. Maxwell
brushes him aside, and the next day the man confronts the congregation with the gap between their lifestyle and Jesus'. Shortly after
making his emotional appeal, the man dies.

Pastor Maxwell is sorely convicted by how little his own life
reflects the generosity of Jesus, and he challenges his congregation
to consider, from that point forward, asking themselves before any
major decision, *What would Jesus do?*

For the rest of the novel, Sheldon explores examples of what that
might look like in action—in the workplace, in the theater, with the
homeless on the streets, and in the halls of government.

Pastor Maxwell's question, of course, has since become quite
famous. During my college years it appeared as a bracelet with the
simple acronym "WWJD." For three full generations this question,
based on Sheldon's 130-year-old novel, has spurred young believers
to think about what following Jesus looks like. Gen Z has added an
accompanying acronym: "HWLF." He would love first.

What would Jesus do? He would love first. Not a bad place to start
in learning to imitate Jesus. It means we enter Babylon seeking not

just to maximize profit but to leverage our power to love, serve, and show grace to others just as Jesus showed it to us. That doesn't preclude making a profit, of course. Profit can benefit everybody.

But for the Christian, behind every opportunity for profit lurks a question: How might I use this opportunity to demonstrate the distinctiveness of Jesus?

Tim Keller relates the story of a young college graduate who moved to New York City and landed a job in one of New York's most prestigious advertising agencies on Madison Avenue, working for a man in his congregation. Shortly after she started, she made a mistake that cost the company tens of thousands of dollars. She expected to be fired by the end of the day. Her boss, however, went to the board asking for patience with her and asked for them to let the consequences for her mistake be given to him because, he said, he should have done a better job preparing her—which was really a stretch and everyone knew it. But on his recommendation, the board gave her another chance.

When this young woman heard what her supervisor had done, she came to him in tears, asking him why he would do something like that, especially for someone as insignificant at the company as she. Such things, she knew, just don't happen on Madison Avenue. "Well," he said, "because you asked: my life was forever altered because of someone who took the blame for me. Jesus took the punishment for my sin and gave me new life, and so now I like to do that for others when I can."[1]

I'm not saying that following Jesus in business means never firing someone. I'm saying that gospel-influenced Christians have an instinct for generosity that seeps its way into relationships sometimes even without their knowing it. Maybe it will be in the way you respond to someone treating you poorly at work—a boss who unfairly snaps at you or a coworker who is rude and condescending. Rather than respond in kind, you slow down long enough to consider that different factors might be influencing their behavior, and your first impulse is compassion rather than revenge.

Carrying yourself with a spirit of mercy doesn't mean excusing wrong behavior or failing to confront when necessary. It means doing so as one forever affected by the tenderness and mercy of Christ.

Unexpected Injections of Grace

The marketplace runs on profit, of course, with the general idea being that we get paid according to the value we add. Every properly functioning economy requires this. As my friend Joby Martin says, "We are saved by grace; we are not employed by grace."[2] Christians recognize that behind this economy, *superseding* it, is an even more fundamental economy, one based on grace.

Jesus taught that his kingdom consists of those who are poor in spirit, which means that they recognize everything they have is a *gift* of grace. The poor in spirit stand in contrast to the "rich in spirit," who think they are *entitled* to everything they have. They also stand in contrast to the "middle class in spirit," who believe they've *earned* what they have. Being poor in spirit changes how you see everything.

I have a friend who started a company now worth more than a billion dollars. He confided to me that he sometimes struggles to know how best to apply this principle. The marketplace, he says, is ruthlessly competitive. He compared succeeding in business to the Olympic 100-meter dash final. The difference between first place and last place in that event is usually in the tenths of a second, sometimes in the *hundredths*. Runners therefore take off anything that could slow them down, even by a hundredth of a second. Restrictive clothing, cumbersome jewelry, or even the wrong kind of socks can mean the difference between first place and sixth place. Success in business is like that, he said: If you want to win, you need to shed anything that takes away your competitive advantage in even the slightest of ways.

But . . . this Christian businessman also knows that God has called his people to run their races *differently*—in ways that demonstrate the glory of their King. After all, in Leviticus, God instructed his people not to glean all the way up to the edges when harvesting their fields, and furthermore, anything they dropped while harvesting was to be left for the poor to pick up. They were to leave profit literally on the ground—profit that their competitors could pick up and turn into better business. By commanding them to leave the corners of their fields unharvested, God was requiring them to give up a certain amount of strategic advantage. Leaving this margin, however, gave God space to work. As with Daniel, it's "God math": Less with God's blessing is more than maximized profit without it.

Let me make clear again, however, that I'm not saying that following Jesus in the marketplace means forgiving every customer's debt or regularly taking the blame for someone else. This is not how the marketplace works, and attempting to live this way would ultimately be bad for everyone. Just as parents who always shield their children from the consequences of their actions in the name of "grace" do them a disservice, so rewriting the language of merit and reward in business, education, or the courtroom would ultimately do a great disservice to the world.

Rather, I'm saying that we should conduct our affairs with an eye toward blessing and leave margin in our budgets to bring that blessing to others, even those who haven't earned it. Furthermore, *under the guidance of the Holy Spirit*, we should look for occasional opportunities to display the radical redemption impulse of the gospel.

Extravagant displays of grace, under the leadership of the Spirit, can be useful in testifying to God's great love. And, of course, even when we do let someone suffer under the consequences of their actions, we never stop loving them, blessing them, and desiring the best for them.

But let me explain "God math" a little more, because some of you googled it when I mentioned it above and you found nothing. It's a principle that God wove into creation, and one he made foundational for walking with him. It's a principle, he said, that would allow us opportunities to demonstrate the beauties of his redemption.

The Sabbath Principle and God Math

We see God math at work in the Sabbath command. When God set up Israel's charter, he commanded them to stop all work one day each week and rest. This was not because they could easily get all their work done in six days. In an agrarian society survival was often a day-by-day, week-by-week affair, and cutting your weekly productivity by a seventh could mean the difference between life and death.

God explained the reason for his Sabbath command in Deuteronomy 5:15:

> "[On the Sabbath] you shall remember that you were a slave in the land of Egypt, and the LORD your God brought you out from there with a mighty hand and an outstretched arm. *Therefore the LORD your God commanded you to keep the Sabbath day.*" (emphasis mine)

God wanted his people to take one day to rest and reflect on the fact that their *greatest* need—deliverance from Egypt—was something God had accomplished *all by himself.* And so, in response, he wanted them to cut their productivity by a seventh to proclaim it to the world: *God is the one who protects and prospers us.*

No other society on earth at the time did this, but God wanted his people to demonstrate the basis of their relationship with God was grace. And God multiplied their productivity on the other six days to make up for what they walked away from on the seventh (Ex. 16:22–26).

Chick-fil-A closes each Sunday. Many restaurant owner-operators say it is simultaneously the most popular and least popular thing they do. People want their chicken strips on Sundays, too. But it provides a day of rest in line with the Creator's design and has been part of what makes Chick-fil-A one of the most popular quick service restaurants in the world.

If you don't believe it's possible to do something like this in your work, test him. I have no doubt you will find him, as so many of us have, faithful to his promises.

You say, "Well, that's about taking a Sabbath, but this chapter is on generosity. What does one have to do with the other?" Well, there's a *principle* at work in the Sabbath command that is as important, I believe, as the command itself. That principle is this: If you obey God first in *everything*, he'll multiply your life in ways that give you an opportunity to credit him with your success. (That multiplication takes many forms, by the way, and they are not always monetary!)

God taught Israel to give the first tenth of all they earned back to him. They didn't do this because they always had an extra 10 percent lying around. They were to give God the *first* tenth of each economic yield as a declaration that they trusted God himself to supply all their needs (Mal. 3:10–11). Many times, they felt as though without that tenth they wouldn't be able to make ends meet—and that was the point! In giving first, they were declaring that they trusted God to provide. Trusting his provision, not seeking to maximize their profits, was the secret of their abundance. When others asked how they made it all work, they would reply, "*I'm* not making it all work. God is. I simply obey God and he makes it all work."

God math: 90 percent *with* God's blessing goes farther than 100 percent *without* it.

And that brings us back to the command to show generosity. Grace and generosity may not make much business sense; it may feel like tying weights to your ankles before you sprint the 100-yard dash. These acts of grace are declarations of faith in God, like the Sabbath and tithe, that God promises to use as channels to multiply blessing in your life. They give you opportunities to demonstrate God math, to point people back to *God*, not your hard work, as the secret of your success.

Put First Things First, and God Will Throw In Second Things

When I left for college, my dad gave me one verse he challenged me to use as a life mantra for any and all decisions I made going forward. The verse was Matthew 6:33:

> "But seek first the kingdom of God and his righteousness, and all these things will be added to you."

"Put God first," my dad said, "and he'll add to you *everything else* that you need for the life he has for you."

C. S. Lewis had a great way of summarizing Matthew 6:33. He said that in life there are first things (God and his priorities) and second things (everything else we need in life). If you put first things first, he said, God promises to provide second things. But when you put second things first, not only will you lose the first things, you'll lose the second things as well.[3] That's Lewis's take on Matthew 6:33, and it's a good one. I've found it to be true in any sphere of life I've applied it to, and it certainly applies to the vocational sphere, too.

The businessperson therefore can "afford" to saddle herself, when God leads, with the generosity of grace, tying that cross around their necks even if it slows them down by a few tenths of a second. They can't afford *not* to. That's because it's God, not the businessman's legs, that ultimately carries him across that finish line.

> He prepares rain for the earth;
> He makes grass grow on the hills.
> He gives to the beasts their food,
> and to the young ravens that cry.
> His delight is not in the strength of the horse,
> nor his pleasure in the legs of a man,
> but the LORD takes pleasure in those who fear him,
> in those who hope in his steadfast love.
> (Ps. 147:8–11)

God is the one who makes it rain. So prioritize displaying his grace.

If Your Life Were a Party . . .

One thing I want to be careful not to imply is that living out the gospel in our lives means merely throwing in a few sporadic moments of grace into an otherwise self-interested pursuit of accumulation. A gospel-shaped approach to our lives goes much deeper than that—it means reshaping our whole approach to life around Jesus' example of servanthood. He came not to be served but to serve.

In Luke 14, Jesus compared living faithfully for the kingdom to throwing a party:

> "When you give a dinner or a banquet, do not invite your friends
> or your brothers or your relatives or rich neighbors, lest they also
> invite you in return and you be repaid. But when you give a feast,

invite the poor, the crippled, the lame, the blind, and you will be blessed, because they cannot repay you. For you will be repaid at the resurrection of the just." (Luke 14:12–14)

Parties in those days were not just social events; they were business affairs. You'd invite the most important people in your circle to your party in the hopes they would invite you to theirs so that you could get to know all their important friends. Party invitations were supposed to be tit-for-tat. So filling up your party with people who couldn't return the favor would have been tantamount to economic suicide.

Jesus' point was not to set out strict parameters for the guest list of our next birthday bash. He was using "banquet" as a metaphor for our lives. "If your life were a party," he was asking, "who are you throwing it for?" Are you investing all your time, treasure, and talent into those who can enrich your life in return, or are you pouring out your life, as Jesus did, for those who cannot repay you?

Christians stand out because they throw the party of their lives for those who will never be able to pay them back.

Is this how you think about the investment of your time, treasure, and talents?

I can't help but think of Eric, a very successful financial adviser in our church. Eric spends an inordinate amount of time each month mentoring and training those who are struggling financially, teaching them how to set up budgets and organize their priorities. Many financial advisers seek to make their money by managing the assets of a few really wealthy clients. Eric has some of those, but he also invests hours and hours into people whose meager portfolios will likely never contribute meaningfully to his bottom line. He thinks of his financial counsel as a ministry, even for his wealthy clients. He helps them think about money in healthy ways and invest it wisely. And, of course, Eric gives away gobs and gobs of his own money for other kingdom work.

Reading Jesus' parable, I often ask myself: Am I looking for an earthly return on everything I do? A lot of times in leadership we talk about investing in people. But doesn't that imply that I'm looking for some kind of personal return from them? A significant portion of my ministry should be spent pouring my time and energy into people who will never really be able to contribute anything back to me personally. We are to love people the way Jesus loved us, to pour ourselves out for them as Jesus poured himself out for us. We were, after all, not too great of an investment for Jesus. Jesus said even the best of us will one day say, "We are unprofitable servants" (Luke 17:10 NKJV).

Christians in Babylon stand out for their periodic departures from calculated investments to self-emptying generosity. Look around the room at the party of their lives and you'll see the poor, crippled, lame, and blind sitting around their tables. Their lives display redemption, and that forces Nebuchadnezzar to pay attention to the ever-generous King of the universe, whose earthly crown was one of thorns and his treasure the joy of his people.

The spirit of the Christian's work is supposed to be *different*. If followers of Jesus are driven by the same motivations as everyone else, we won't stand out! And if we're not different, we can't make a difference.

The days of our lives are to bless others, not just enrich ourselves. We leverage our prosperity more to increase our standard of giving than to increase our standard of living!

CHAPTER|12

Mission-Advancing

I have become all things to all people,
that by all means I might save some. I
do it all for the sake of the gospel.
—1 CORINTHIANS 9:22–23

I have but one passion: It is [Christ], it is he alone.
The world is the field and the field is the world; and
henceforth that country shall be my home where I
can be most used in winning souls for Christ.
—COUNT NIKOLAUS LUDWIG VON ZINZENDORF

The start of every *Mission Impossible* movie finds Ethan Hunt, played by Tom Cruise, opening a suspicious-looking package with instructions for a harrowing mission to save humanity from some sinister villain hell-bent on causing a global catastrophe.

It's never an easy mission, of course—otherwise the movie series would have been called *Entirely Possible and Only Mildly Interesting Missions*. The missions require Hunt to drive a hundred miles an hour down crowded European streets, jump between roofs of downtown London skyscrapers, dangle off train cars teetering on the edge of collapsing bridges, and, of course, run full speed for a sustained time through back alleys and crowded malls. All the while exchanging coolheaded, witty banter with the good-looking, perfectly manicured model who somehow got trapped beside him during his daring escapade. You know, really relatable stuff.

It's easy to overlook that followers of Jesus are given instructions for a mission no less urgent and far more important than anything ever given to Ethan Hunt. And one even more impossible. Unlike Hunt's instructions, however, ours didn't self-destruct in our hands the moment we read them. The gospel of Matthew records Jesus' final words on earth, what Christians call "the Great Commission":

> "Go therefore and make disciples of all nations, baptizing them in the name of the Father and of the Son and of the Holy Spirit, teaching them to observe all that I have commanded you." (Matt. 28:19–20)

And that brings us to the fifth quality of our remarkable, beautiful, quiet life: mission-advancing.

The Only Verb in Our Great Commission

We saw in a previous chapter that there's only one verb in the Great Commission: *mathēteusate*—"Make disciples," which means that everything else the church does centers on, and flows out of, our primary assignment of disciple making.

It's an assignment given to every Christian, not just a few specially called super Christians. I used to think that calling into ministry was a sacred privilege reserved for a select few, bestowed by a mystical manifestation. For years I embraced what I call the "Cheerios method" of discerning the call of God—if God was calling you into his service, he'd do something mystical such as spell out a message in your Cheerios: *Be a missionary. Teach Sunday school.* For the record, I stared at my Cheerios for years and all they ever spelled out was *Oooooooooooo.*

The truth is that *every* Christian is called into ministry. The call to ministry is *included* in the call to follow Jesus. In Matthew 4:19 Jesus said to his first followers, "Follow me, and I will make you fishers of men." This means when you accepted the call to follow Jesus, you accepted the call to mission. The question now is no longer *if* you are called—it's where and how.

The Great Commission Jesus gave to the disciples assumes we are already going somewhere. The original Greek language says "as you are going." It's not just a command for a few of us to *start* going somewhere, it's an acknowledgment that we're all already headed somewhere. *As you go* to the office. *As you go* to school. *As you go* to the coffee shop. *As you go* to your Zumba class. Your work, family, school, neighborhood, and soccer pitch are your mission fields. You don't have to hop on a plane to Zambia to engage in the Great Commission. Some of us should, but that wasn't all Jesus had in mind when he spoke those words.

You might argue that Christians in the marketplace today have greater access to unreached places than anyone else. Urbanization, market globalization, and revolutions in technology have given the professional community nearly universal access to people everywhere.

The 10/40 ~~Window~~ Door

Many Christians have found they possess skills that can take them into places around the world where there is little to no gospel influence. Missiologists refer to something called the "10/40 window," which refers to the area of the globe between 10 degrees south and 40 degrees north of the equator. These regions, comprising sixty-nine countries, are home to nearly four billion people, almost half of whom have never heard the first word of gospel proclamation. The

10/40 window is also home to millions of the world's most impoverished people.[1]

Years ago I read that there were around 40,000 evangelical missionaries (counting all Protestant denominations) working in the 10/40 window. And that's great—we need four times that many! But get this: The number of US citizens working in secular jobs in the 10/40 window right now, according to the US Department of State, is *2,000,000*. Around 24 percent of those individuals identify themselves as "born-again Christians."[2] Let's assume that half of that 24 percent are not too serious about their faith. That still leaves more than 200,000 committed followers of Jesus who got up this morning to work a job in the least reached part of the planet. What if those 200,000 had been trained by their churches to see their primary calling as a disciple-making disciple? Wouldn't that mean our mission force in the 10/40 window would surge from 40,000 to 240,000— without costing the church another dime?

Our failure to complete the Great Commission has nothing to do with a resource shortage; it has to do with believers not understanding their primary commission and failing to leverage their careers for the reason God gave them. Remember, God put us in Babylon not to build personal shiny and comfortable little kingdoms for ourselves but to testify to a coming kingdom that will one day fill the earth.

Missiologist Mike Barnett, in his book *Discovering the Mission of God*, points out that if you lay a map of global poverty over a map of world evangelization, you'll see that the poorest places on the planet are also the least reached by the gospel. The least evangelized places are simultaneously those in greatest need of business development. That turns the 10/40 window into a *door*. Barnett continues:

> Though 20% of the world's population lives in Muslim countries, only 4% of world trade comes from these countries. . . . We are living at a point in world history of unprecedented opportunities

for the expansion of the Christian faith. No country is closed to business. In no country is it illegal to love people. There are huge doors of opportunity wide open before us, if we are willing to equip ourselves adequately and walk through them. Countries considered "closed" to missionaries welcome Christians who come as [businesspeople].[3]

Consider, for example, the country of Iran. Iran is one of the least reached places in the world, and one of the least welcoming countries on earth to do missionary work. But out of 90 million people there, only 13.4 million have full-time jobs.[4] That means entrepreneurial businesspeople have an opportunity that full-time pastors and missionaries do not.

I realize not everyone reading this has the ability to use their career this way. But some do. Who knows whether *you* have come into the kingdom for just such a time as this?

At our church we tell all our college graduates: Following Jesus means doing whatever you do *well* to the glory of God and doing it *somewhere strategic* for the mission of God. Lots of factors go into where you choose to pursue your career—things such as strength of the job market there, proximity of family and friends, desirability of the city—and those are all valid. But for citizens of heaven, why wouldn't the weightiest of all of those factors be where you can be part of something strategic in God's mission?

You have to get a job *somewhere*, so why not get a job in a place where you can be part of something strategic King Jesus is doing? Remember, you're just an exile here. So arrange your life according to what is most advantageous for Jesus' kingdom. If we have freedom to move around in Babylon, we should make those moves based on what is in the best interests of our home country.

Thinking this way brings God's blessing; failing to do so invites his curse. In the Old Testament, after Abraham and his nephew Lot decided they needed to part ways so that each would have ample room to feed their flocks, Lot chose a direction solely on the basis of where business would be best for him. He did not even factor in kingdom interests. Well, if you know the rest of Lot's story, you know it didn't turn out that great for him. Things got pretty salty. Don't be Lot.

There is a young man in our church whom I'll call Ryan who made a better choice. Ryan graduated from an elite university with a degree in sports marketing. He was immediately recruited by one of the nation's top marketing firms, a firm with a large headquarters in our area. Over the course of a couple of years, Ryan progressed upward in the company, but God was also giving Ryan a heart for the nations. Ryan did a little digging and found out his company had a remote office in a place where we were planting a church in the Middle East. He asked his boss whether there was a possibility of being transferred there. His boss told him that was crazy—up-and-comers don't take remote positions in the developing world. Ryan asked to be transferred anyway. He joined our church-planting team, fully self-supported. After a few years he resigned from his firm and started his own marketing firm in that region, where he began supporting others on the team, too.

I think of what my own parents did in their retirement. As I explained earlier, my dad worked for forty years as an executive in a multinational company based out of Winston-Salem, North Carolina. The day he retired, his company *rehired* him to oversee the building of a textile plant *in a city right in the middle of the 10/40 window*! There he and my mom rubbed shoulders with Asian businesspeople whom I (as a pastor) would never be able to get close to on a short-term mission trip giving out water bottles and evangelistic tracts. While there, they had the privilege of leading a man to Christ and working with a local church planter to help get a church started there, right in the heart of the 10/40 window.

Total cost to the church? Zero dollars.

In fact, the church made money on the deal because my parents kept tithing back home while they were there.

God wants his people to put down roots in Babylons around the world, to get jobs there, to get spooky good at those jobs, and then to leverage the opportunities provided by those jobs to point people to Jesus.

> Do you see a man skillful in his work?
> He will stand before kings. (Prov. 22:29)

Believers who do their work well to the glory of God and do it somewhere strategic for the mission of God will fulfill the Great Commission. Their excellence in business will give them audiences with the kings and influencers in the most unreached places in the world.

Your secular skill might be the key that opens some nation or people group to the gospel.

So do your work, but don't forget the mission.

The mission is the most important thing. It's why he has us here in exile, in Babylon. Not to make a fortune in it but to be a light to it.

And as we'll see, that worked out for Daniel in an incredible way.

"Daniel Told Us About a King"

Shortly after Jesus was born, a group of "wise men from the east" (Matt. 2:1) showed up claiming to have seen a star announcing the birth of a promised king. We always assume there were three men, though the fact that their arrival troubled the whole city suggests that this might have been a much bigger group than three. Either way, scholars say that their title indicates they were part of the Persian ruling class.[5]

How had they known what this mysterious star meant?

Well, remember, Persia was a region where Daniel had lived in exile. Evidently Daniel had shared the Torah, Moses' writings, with the wise men of the region, which would have included this prophecy: "A star shall come out of Jacob, and a scepter shall rise out of Israel" (Num. 24:17).

A few hundred years later a generation of Persian wise men saw a mysterious star in the heavens, and when they consulted the Torah, they saw that it announced the birth of a king, the one Daniel had told them about. And they came to worship.

That sheds a new light on God's promise that if Daniel did his job well, he would shine in Babylon "like the stars forever and ever," doesn't it?

Daniel and his friends had been carted off into exile against their wills. Their work in the palace surely included a lot of mundane, secular Babylonian tasks. But they excelled at what they did, and they never forgot that their primary assignment was to testify to a coming King of Israel. And testify they did.

You Had One Job

Toward the end of a sermon one week I called five unsuspecting people onstage. I told them they were going to act out the various jobs of firemen on a fire truck. I made one the driver and another the supervisor and had two operate the hose and one drive the back of the truck (the tiller). Then I asked each of them what their primary role was on this truck. Each one dutifully repeated back the job I had assigned them. I then told each of them they were wrong.

Their *primary* role? To put out fires.

It wasn't a fair question; I had set them up. But it illustrated an important point about the Great Commission. Our "participles"—working, playing, living—all spring from one verb—"Make disciples." That's our central commission.

What might that look like with your "participles"? I have a friend who runs a business, and he hosts special lunches around major Christian holidays (Good Friday, Christmas Eve) in which he facilitates a special testimony time, gives a Bible study, or brings in someone to share their testimony. It's amazing who shows up for these things. I know of another guy who runs a software company and uses a portion of his profits to contract technicians in India to give their opinions on a special translation of the gospel of Mark as a kind of market research. He hosts online discussion groups to analyze feedback. It has led to all kinds of gospel conversations. I know of others who simply make a habit of making the rounds in their "cubicle farm" each week looking for opportunities to pray for coworkers and stay invested in their lives.

These same principles apply outside the workplace, too. Take, for example, your local public school. God intends for us to be a light there, too, to bless it and make it better, not just condemn it from a distance. For in its prosperity you will find your own prosperity.

The North American Mission Board lists the following five ways Christians in Babylon can make a gospel impact in their public education system:

1. **ADOPT TEACHERS:** "Hold a bake sale to raise money for classroom supplies. Provide breakfast for department meetings. Send them pick-me-ups and treats during finals week or the vacation-less stretch between Labor Day and Thanksgiving. Ask for loads you can lighten. Plan as many touches as possible, each time building relational equity."

2. **BE THE GO-TO:** "Schools are often the first to know when kids and their families go through hardships and calamities. Contact school leadership, volunteering your church as a first-call when needs arise. Maybe your building could serve as a shelter when freezing temperatures get dangerous.

Set up a Wi-Fi network to give kids access to the internet to complete assignments. Assist the school in stocking and running a clothes closet. Find out if a school family needs help getting the water turned back on. Meet tangible needs to create relationships that can meet our great eternal need."

3. **SUPPORT STUDENTS:** "Reach out to a school principal and volunteer your time to meet with at-risk students. . . . Does your church have a wealth of faithful men who led their families well? What about older women who can speak wisdom? Enlist these older saints to join you and provide stability, dependability, and Godly influence in a young person's life."

4. **CHAPLAIN A TEAM:** "Coaches know their players and speak into their lives in a way that isn't always possible or welcome in a classroom environment. . . . Volunteer as an assistant coach or as a logistics coordinator. Get to know the coach and the players. Be there for the thrill of victory and the agony of defeat . . . and look for open doors."

5. **FLOOD THE SCHOOL WITH YOUR PEOPLE:** "What church wouldn't jump at the chance to have missionaries from their pews embedded into a mission field—and to have them be paid for it? Under the right circumstances, retirees, stay-at-home moms of school-age kids, and church staff are all potential 'missionaries' to be sent into public schools. And, when they're there, they need to do whatever they are tasked to do—clean bathrooms, file paperwork, follow sub plans—do it to the glory of God!"[6]

I offer these as examples to get your thinking going. Ideas for this kind of engagement are as diverse as the work and education environments we find ourselves in. I don't know exactly what it will look like for you in Babylon, but God has something for you there, I assure you.

Remember, the only verb of the Great Commission, and the primary verb of your life, is *make disciples*. This is what you do *as you go*, wherever you are going. *It's why you are where you are.* To do good work—excellent work, God-glorifying work—and, through that, to direct people's attention to Jesus.

Thirty-nine of the forty miracles described in the book of Acts took place outside the church. God has more miracles to do in your Babylon.

Ask the Holy Spirit for wisdom, then step out and take a risk.

PART 3

Testify
Loudly

In part 2 we discussed the quiet, beautiful, gently subversive gospel-centered life of the Christian in exile.

Part 3 takes us into the loud parts.

If part 2 highlights the "everyday" aspects of the Christian life, these chapters take us into the "revolutionary" impact a quiet life sets us up for.

A quiet life and a loud testimony are not contradictions. The quietness itself is quite loud; quietly kneeling when others stand, quietly doing our best work regardless of who notices, quietly showing up for the funeral of a family member of someone who has been unkind to you, or quietly forgoing vengeance.

Conducting ourselves with meekness, gentleness, and respect (1 Peter 3:4, 15) and turning the world upside down (Acts 17:6) go hand in hand. The former sets you up for the latter. In this section I want to give you five ways you can turn up the volume that will amplify your witness in Babylon:

- Loud courage
- Loud joy
- Loud generosity
- Loud hospitality
- Let heaven get loud

CHAPTER | 13

Loud Courage

Our God whom we serve is able to deliver us from
the burning fiery furnace, and he will deliver us
out of your hand, O king. But if not, be it known
to you, O king, that we will not serve your gods or
worship the golden image that you have set up.
—DANIEL 3:17–18

You may not recognize the name Desmond Doss, but you might have seen the movie about his life, *Hacksaw Ridge*. At the beginning of World War 2, Doss was drafted into the US Army. He deeply loved and wanted to serve his country, but being a pacifist, he couldn't bring himself to train with a weapon. Rather than opt out of the draft, he trained as a medic.

Fellow soldiers mocked him mercilessly. That is, until one evening when the Japanese pinned down his unit on top of a cliff in Okinawa. Many in his unit had been killed, but several of the wounded were stranded underneath the incessant and withering gunfire. Doss knew that if the wounded were left up on that ridge overnight, most would die. Because of their position on the cliff, however, it was impossible for rescue units to get up there without becoming casualties themselves. Doss rigged up a stretcher that could be lowered by a series of ropes to the ground below, then Doss, all by himself, retrieved every single wounded soldier. It was incredible. He saved the lives of seventy-five men that night.

At the war's conclusion President Truman recognized Doss as one of the bravest warriors of World War 2 and did something never done before or since in our military: He presented the Congressional Medal of Honor, our country's most prestigious military service award, to a man who never picked up a weapon.

The greatest things in the world happen through courage. Lots of us dream of making a great impact on the world. Without courage, however, we'll never do it.

The philosopher Aristotle famously said that courage is the most important of all the virtues, because without courage we'll never persist in any of the others. Honesty doesn't serve you that well, for example, if you fold every time the pressure is on. C. S. Lewis concurred, saying, "Courage is not simply one of the virtues, but the form of *every* virtue at the testing point."[1]

I'm not sure whether any virtue is more essential for exiles in Babylon than courage.

We've Been Here Before

Historians regard the persecution of Caesar Diocletian at the conclusion of the third century to be the worst concentrated period of Christian persecution in history. Diocletian mandated that every Roman subject obtain a *libellus* ("permission to sell") to buy or sell in the marketplace. To obtain that *libellus*, one had to go down to a Roman government building, take a pinch of incense and offer it on an altar to Caesar, saying "Dominus Caesar" ("Caesar is Lord"). It was a rather ingenious way, on Diocletian's part, to smoke out hidden Christians, whom he knew would only say "Dominus Iesus" ("Jesus is Lord").

166

I can only imagine how difficult it must have been for Christian fathers who knew that not making the offering amounted to a choice not to feed their families. "It's only words," some probably told themselves. "I don't have to *mean* them."

Many refused to make the offering, however. It was a dark and terrible chapter in the church's history. And yet the bravery of that generation sustained the church. The steadfast devotion of Christians in that generation led, in fact, to the conversion of Emperor Constantine, who in 312 issued the Edict of Milan which eventually made Christianity the official religion of the Roman Empire.

I think it's safe to say that you and I are reading this book because a generation of Christians refused to make the pinch and say the words.

What will happen when our generation is tested this way?

As Christian morality gets pushed further and further outside the Overton window, we are likely to see business owners face tax penalties, fines, and even seizures for not going along with Nebuchadnezzar's agenda. I'm not trying to be an alarmist or embracing a Christian-persecution complex; it's just hard to deny that that's where we're headed.[2]

The easy part will be taking the stand and proclaiming loyalty to Christ. That part might even feel good! The hard part will be dealing with the fallout—like trying to figure out how to feed your family after you've been fired. (In the words of the infamous Russian dissident Alexei Navalny, "It is easier to perform a bold action than to live with its consequences!"[3])

And that means many of us may have to ask something of ourselves that our most recent forebears didn't have to ask, at least not to the degree we may have to:

If prospering in God's kingdom means struggling in Nebuchadnezzar's, am I okay with that?

For a while citizens of God's kingdom in the West have been able to prosper in both. That may be changing.

Daring to Be a Daniel

"Dare to be a Daniel" was the challenge my Sunday school teacher gave whenever she walked us through the flannel-graph lesson on the life of Daniel, because the need for courage appears at nearly every turn in his story.

As you recall from part 1 of this book, Daniel and his teenage friends courageously refused to eat from the king's forbidden delicacies, then courageously refused to bow before Nebuchadnezzar's golden statue, then courageously explained to Nebuchadnezzar the truth about the wickedness of his ways, then courageously delivered to him the bad news about his future, then courageously continued to pray to God with the windows open three times every day even after the king had forbidden it.

Esther's story as an exile is also one framed by courage. She had to walk into the court of the most powerful and misogynistic king in the world and tell him that he was wrong, a king known to order exiles and executions at the slightest annoyance.

Peter and Paul both courageously died as martyrs, the former by upside-down crucifixion and the latter by beheading, for refusing to compromise with Babylon.

Maybe you don't think of yourself as a naturally courageous person. For most of us, courage is something we have to *learn*. C. S. Lewis said that a lack of courage was probably his greatest weakness, too, and something he had devoted considerable parts of his life to developing. Honestly, that encourages me. I've always found preaching about courage easy; living it has been more difficult.

Daniel's story teaches us a lot about courage—both why it's

needed and where it comes from. It's helpful for those of us with a natural tendency to avoid conflict and go with the flow.

Courage's Testing Point

Daniel's story shows us that courage's testing point is not found in our private expressions of faith. For the most part, Daniel was allowed to live and let live in Babylon. Where things got squirrely was when Daniel dared to deny Nebuchadnezzar's overarching authority.

The second chapter of Daniel reveals that Nebuchadnezzar was not upset that Daniel and his friends worshiped the God of Israel—in fact, he gave them express permission to do so.[4] Nebuchadnezzar was upset, rather, that they would not acknowledge his gods, too. Just before the famous "fiery furnace" scene in Daniel 3, Nebuchadnezzar publicly acknowledged the legitimacy of Daniel's God, literally *bowing down* to him (Dan. 2:46)! It seems only fair, then, that they also acknowledge his god—after all, that's how a pluralistic society works, right? You acknowledge mine and I acknowledge yours?

It was not what Daniel and his friends *affirmed* that was the problem, but what they dared to deny.

In the same way, we won't get in too much trouble today for saying that Jesus is our *personal* Savior. It's when we fail to affirm that salvation is found by other means, too, or when we say that Jesus is Lord over what we think or what we do with our bodies.

Just a few years ago it was reported that the dean at Stanford University forced a group of Christian students to stop proselytizing on Stanford's campus.[5] He told them it was fine for them to gather together as often as they wanted for worship, but they were not allowed to try to persuade others that salvation was found only in their Jesus, because he said that one of Stanford's core principles was that all faiths are equally valid as religions. In other words, it's fine for Christians to worship Jesus, but they cannot deny that these other gods are also worthy of worship. We can bow down to Jesus, but we also must bow down to the gigantic statue of pluralism.

As we've seen, Christians in the early church were asked to play by the same rules. Rome, it has been said, had only two basic religious rules for its empire:

1. Worship any god you want. You can continue to worship your tribal or regional gods, visit their temples, and make offerings to them.
2. Don't say your god is the only god, or the supreme god, because then you'll think that you, as his people, should rule with him.[6]

We experience the same kind of pressure to present God's moral law as one option among many. Our society says, "You Christians are free to practice marriage God's way if you want, but how dare you label someone else's choices as *sin*? We demand that you acknowledge the rightness of our lifestyle by displaying this flag during pride week. If not, we'll cancel you on social media, boycott your business, remove your tax-exempt status, and shut you down." Sometimes it feels easier just to keep our heads down, make the offering, and go along.

God put us into Babylon not to practice our private morality behind closed doors, however, but to put him on display in broad daylight. That means there are times we must fling open the windows and say, "We kneel before God and God alone, and we'll do it every day in every circumstance."

Kneeling before God in the privacy of your bedroom doesn't take a lot of courage. Flinging open the windows does.

As citizens in Babylon, we're not called to force others to adopt our beliefs, but we are called to provide clear and faithful testimony to our King. We cannot affirm what God has forbidden, even as we acknowledge that in a secular society citizens have been granted license for a while to live as they wish.

All our society really wants right now is for us to affirm that they have the authority to make whatever moral choices they want to make, to acknowledge that their will is Lord ("Dominus voluntas mea"), and to bow before the golden statue of their self-sovereignty. This is an authority we can never affirm.

That will take courage, and we should expect to suffer for it. When we do, we should not be discouraged, because that moment of suffering is the very thing Jesus intends to use as his vehicle to demonstrate his all-surpassing worth in the eyes of watching Babylonians.

Courage Creates the Moment for Jesus to Shine

It was only after Shadrach, Meshach, and Abednego, Daniel's friends, were thrown into the fiery furnace that God showed up in breathtaking ways. It's a heart-stopping scene:

> Then King Nebuchadnezzar was astonished and rose up in haste. He declared to his counselors, "Did we not cast three men bound into the fire?" They answered and said to the king, "True, O king." He answered and said, "But I see four men unbound, walking in the midst of the fire, and they are not hurt; and the appearance of the fourth is *like a son of the gods.*" (Dan. 3:24–25, emphasis mine)

News flash for Nebuchadnezzar! *It was the Son of God.* The Son of God stood with his people when they stood for him, and he showed up for them when they showed up for him.

I love the idea of Jesus showing off his power through me in a moment like this, but honestly, I *hate being in the circumstances* that require it. Those circumstances represent some of my greatest fears. I don't like to be unpopular, alone, or seen as backward. I don't like to be boycotted or have my livelihood threatened. But God put us here to show off his distinctiveness, and, well, you can't make a difference unless you are different.

Our being different bothers Babylonians. Sometimes they want to throw us in the lions' den for it.

Daniel knew exactly what was at stake when he flung open those windows to pray toward Jerusalem (Dan. 6:10). Someone might have said to him, "But, Daniel, you can pray without opening your windows! Nothing in Scripture says you have to open your windows to pray." Daniel knew, however, that to not open his windows would be perceived as a retreat from God's authority. It would imply that the culture's authority was more binding than God's.

What does our retreat from talking about unpopular things say to our culture about the "Godship" of God in our lives? When we fly the flags Babylon tells us to fly and stay silent on the things they've told us to keep quiet on, what do we imply about *God's* authority?

Do you want God to be glorified in your workplace, your school, your neighborhood? The power that shuts the mouths of lions is not found in the private expression of our faith in our homes, small groups, or churches. It's found when we fling open the windows and kneel before God publicly. It comes when we speak light into darkness, truth into error, and righteousness into the face of injustice.

Paul knew that faithful Christian testimony, while potent, would also be *unpopular*. That's why he predicted that our message would be to some a fragrance of life and to others a stench of death. People don't like the smell of death, and they'll want to rid themselves of it.

Paul knew if he tried to make the gospel more palatable by the wisdom and eloquence of his age (which in our day might include celebrating individuality and downplaying the sinfulness of alternate sexualities), he likely would gain a more eager audience, but the cross he preached would be divested of its power (1 Cor. 2:4). The Spirit of God flows only through the conduit of truth.

At the center of the preaching of the cross, you see, is a command to repentance. The lordship of Jesus, properly understood, is the *most* offensive thing there is. It is way more offensive than any conviction on sexuality. It requires that you surrender your perspective on *everything* to him. Jesus once told a crowd that to follow him meant denying themselves, taking up their crosses, and following him with no conditions or caveats (Matt. 16:24). What he said was offensive. So offensive, in fact, that many people stopped following him when he said that!

Becket Cook, a gay man who was working in Hollywood's entertainment industry when he became a Christian, explains how Jesus' demand for self-denial cut against the grain of his soul: "All my life I'd been told to be true to myself." But in reading the Bible, he saw something else:

> [The self] is corrupted by sin, so why be true to that? The whole idea of [choosing your sexuality] is bound to the exaltation of self. It carries the implication of making yourself your own god. Putting yourself and your desires on a pedestal and worshiping them. Being true to yourself is nothing short of idolatry.[7]

Repentance is not merely changing your mind about homosexuality; repentance means denying our society's core claim that we are the ones in the best position to decide what is right for ourselves.

Babylonians will accept our message not when we sufficiently tailor it to their liking but when God changes their hearts so they can hear it. He works that change only through bold, uncompromising testimony, never clever, message-altering marketing.

The Aroma of Life in Hollywood

A guy who works closely with me now at our church, Brian, also previously lived and worked in Hollywood. He got a job at the writers' guild there, taking the place of an assistant who had just been fired. Normally, he said, when someone gets fired at the writers' guild, security wipes their computer and resets their station *immediately*, but this woman's workstation sat idle for several days. Finally, the supervisor asked Brian to make sure there was nothing that needed to be saved and then reset it.

The woman had been a zealous LGBT advocate, and open on her desktop was some correspondence from an LGBT discussion group she was a part of. "In this correspondence," Brian told me, "they were complaining about *you*. Apparently you had spoken at a conference where several members of this group had attended, and they were talking about what a kind person you had been to them, but then you'd surprised them by saying that homosexuality was sinful and contrary to God's design. They said you were the most dangerous kind of person—kind and generous on the outside but bigoted and hateful on the inside. The fact that you 'acted like' you cared about them only made it worse because people wouldn't realize you were so dangerous."

Brian told me that he was intrigued by the description of the message I had given because although he had struggled with same-sex attraction for years, he was also interested in Jesus. He wasn't sure whether the former disqualified him permanently from the latter. He'd always thought, "I can never belong to Jesus if I am attracted to other men. If I can ever overcome that, maybe he'll have me."

Brian had made multiple attempts to transform himself into a person who would be "worthy" of the love of Jesus, but all his attempts had failed. By this point in his life, he said, he'd given up hope and was contemplating suicide. Later that evening, he looked me up and started listening to messages from our church. He said, "For the first time in my life I heard that I didn't have to make myself worthy enough for Jesus; he accepted me just as I was, even the mess that I was. I had known about Jesus before, but this was the first time I understood how he felt about me."

To make a long story short, through the help of a Christian friend and local church there, he accepted Christ. He then bought a plane ticket and flew out to Raleigh, came to one of our weekend services, walked up to me, introduced himself, and said, "I came all this way because I wanted to say thank you. Thank you," he said, "for being courageous enough to stick to the truth and gracious enough to make me not feel cast aside forever." He then gave me this letter:

I heard you preach on the cross, and you explained that Jesus took away all our guilt and shame by bearing it himself; that we're not just forgiven, we're made pure by the blood of Christ . . . and then, for the first time, it all began to make sense.

My same-sex desires don't define me. My identity is now built on something so much greater—my resurrected Savior Jesus Christ and how he feels about me.

God knew me from before the foundation of the world, he knew my sin, he knew what my struggles would be, and he still chose to send his Son to live the perfect life I could never live and die the death that I deserved. On the cross, he traded places with me, taking my sin and shame and giving me his place of righteousness with the Father. Now, even with my same-sex desire, I am in Christ; I am a new creation.

I began to see my struggle with SSA [same-sex attraction] as a way to draw closer to Christ—as a way for me to see my own sinfulness and be driven even more to treasure the gospel, to treasure the fact that in Christ I'm fully known and fully loved.

The thought of eternity has become so much sweeter—knowing that, even if I struggle in this world for the rest of my life, one day I'll be with my Savior and be completely freed from this and every sin. Forever. It's almost too good to be true.

All of that is to say thank you for being relentlessly committed to the gospel. I'm proof that faithfulness to the gospel in this area is crucial. At a fragile time in my life, when I could have been driven to despair or to an abandonment of Christian faith, I heard, submitted to, and treasured the gospel, and I thank you and the Summit Church for your role in that.

A few years later he moved to go to a local seminary and become a part of our church. Whenever I look over at him on Sunday morning, his hands raised in worship, tears often filling his eyes, I'm reminded of the importance of courage. Life change doesn't happen through a compromised message. The power of Jesus' Spirit rests on the simple testimony of Christ's lordship, preached without apology. People-pleasing message editing may win society's approval for a minute, but courage wins friends for eternity.

It's time for us to throw open the windows, turn our faces toward Jerusalem, and lift our hands in faith to God. It's time to stop being afraid. The God who shuts the mouths of lions is ready to help.

Let's Get Practical

It's easy to get inspired by the above and resolve to be more courageous. But through countless conversations with people in the workplace, boardrooms, classrooms, and PTA meetings, I know a lot of times we're just not sure what courage looks like in practice in a pluralistic society. Which issues do you take public stands on? When do you throw open the windows? What's the difference between living alongside people in Babylon, respecting their rights in a pluralistic society, and implicitly condoning their errors? What do courage and faithfulness look like in a world with pronoun preferences, tolerance protocols, and corporate social-responsibility indexes?

First, let's acknowledge that these issues were tough even for one as courageous and righteous as Daniel. I'll give you just one example: what Daniel had to do about his name.

Daniel and his friends had good Hebrew names that high-lighted their faith in God. After they arrived in Babylon, however, Nebuchadnezzar changed their names to give praise to his gods.

- Daniel's name, which meant "God is my judge," got changed to Belteshazzar, which meant "Baal protects the king."
- Hananiah, "God is gracious," got changed to Shadrach, "under the command of Aku, the moon god."
- Mishael, "There is none like God," got changed to Meshach, "There is none like Aku."
- Azariah, "God has helped me," got changed to Abed-Nego, "the servant of Nebo" (the god of wisdom).

Every time Daniel answered to "Belteshazzar," he probably felt as though he was, in some way, affirming error. Daniel had made it clear, in multiple places, whose servant he really was and that he was ready to die rather than compromise obedience to his God. Yet Daniel answered when called "Belteshazzar." Life in Babylon felt messy, I'm sure!

Let me offer an example from another sphere: My friend Russell, who lives in Germany, faces a dilemma each year when he pays taxes there. One of the questions on the tax form asks if you are a Christian. If you check yes, you then indicate whether you are Catholic or Lutheran, and an 8 percent tax is added to your tax levy. Russell goes weekly to an unaffiliated Baptist church. So he has to check no each year on the tax form, even though he knows that the German government has confused and corrupted the label "Christian."

Sheesh. This is the messiness of living in Babylon! Is there any guidance?

The Courage Sextant

In 1982, Steve Callahan found himself stranded at sea on a small raft in the middle of the Atlantic after a catastrophic boating accident. Though weak and disoriented, he managed to tie together three pencils to create a makeshift sextant, a device that uses the fixed points of the sun, the horizon, and the time of day to help navigate the ocean. Using those three reference points, he determined his latitude, caught the right current, and eventually drifted to safety in the Caribbean after seventy-six days at sea.

Let me suggest three fixed reference points that can serve as a makeshift sextant for you when navigating the treacherous waters of moral faithfulness in Babylon.

Reference Point 1: We Are Called to _Participate_ in "the Commons"

Christian ethicists since Augustine have referred to something they call "the commons," which denotes the secular space where Christians are called to live and work, the kingdoms of this world where God's name is often not known or his authority recognized. We are called, as the prophet Jeremiah said, to do life and business there and to bless its inhabitants whether they share our convictions or not.

Our responsibility as believers is to put our products and services into the commons indiscriminately, for the blessing of all. What unbelievers do with them from there is not our responsibility. Like

Jesus said of the heavenly Father, we make our "sun" shine and our "rain" fall on both the just and the unjust (Matt. 5:45). Jesus' famous story illustrating what it looks like to love our neighbors, the parable of the good Samaritan, features a man who showed kindness to a person of a different race and religion. If the unjust use the warmth of our "sun" and the nourishment of our "rain" to grow crops of sin, that's not on us.

For example, if a Christian construction developer builds a neighborhood and an unmarried, cohabiting couple buys one of the homes, the developer is not guilty of assisting that couple in their sin by providing a home to sin in. Christian ethicists agree that it would be wrong for the developer *not* to sell the home to that couple. In the same way, the Christian public-school teacher who helps the atheist student become the best possible writer she can be is not assisting the enemy. She's blessing the citizens of Babylon as God has commanded.

Reference Point 2: We Must Never Fellowship with Sin

At the same time, we have a responsibility *not* to participate with people *in their sin* even as we live and work alongside them in the commons. In Ephesians, God commands us not to go along with the works of darkness but rather to rebuke them (Eph. 5:11). That means we cannot affirm or directly assist people in sin even as we love them, befriend them, employ them, provide services for them, and even develop products that may be used in ways that do not glorify God.

For example, a Christian employer might in good conscience employ someone who intends to have an abortion and provide the salary by which the person pays for the abortion. But to drive the person to the procedure or throw a party celebrating it when it's done would be to fellowship with the works of darkness. There's a difference between befriending a sinner and directly assisting them in their sin. Living as Jesus did, full of grace and truth, means always doing the former but never doing the latter.

I have a friend who told me he couldn't go to a gay work friend's wedding ceremony because he didn't see any way that his presence wouldn't imply affirmation of the ceremony itself. He said, "When the officiant says, 'If any person here knows a reason why these two cannot be united in holy matrimony, let them speak now or forever hold their peace,' what am I supposed to do? Silence implies consent, so I figured it was best for me just not to be there. I told my gay friends that I cared about them and wanted to continue being a part of their lives, but I cannot celebrate or go to their wedding." How my friend is posturing himself captures, I believe, the grace-and-truth balance Jesus tells us to live with.

You could apply this same thinking to the question of whether to use someone's preferred pronouns after they've transitioned to another gender. I know some Christians who believe they can never use the new pronoun because it affirms a lie and goes along with the works of darkness. I know others who believe that after they've made clear that they do not believe it is possible to change one's God-given gender, for the sake of keeping the conversation open they can find a workaround. One explained it this way: "The answer to the question of whether I used someone's preferred pronouns starts and ends with no. In the middle, however, the place where you keep the conversation or relationship going, there is space for accommodation of error without affirmation of it."

These are challenging questions. My counsel would be to always err on the side of clarity and courage.

Reference Point 3: Our Testimony Must Be Full of Grace and Truth

Let me refer back to a concept from a previous chapter: As followers of Jesus, we must be filled with grace and truth.

Every decision we make about how to engage those who don't share our convictions should be looked at through the lens of both.

We're always trying to do two things: (1) fulfill our responsibility to clearly testify to the truth, and (2) do our best to stay in relationship with the person. If we're getting the balance right, we'll speak so clearly that they want to throw us in the lions' den, but they'll also weep at the thought that we'd be gone, because nobody has ever loved them like we've loved them.

Our goal is to engage difficult issues in ways that engage the hearts of Babylonians, following our Savior as he courageously speaks truth and then lays down his life in love for those seeking to kill him.

Courage Comes from an Empty Tomb

As I said, these waters can be a little murky and we should be gracious with one another as we attempt to figure it all out. Just keep in mind our overarching goal in Babylon: to provide a faithful witness to the distinctiveness of Christ and his kingdom. Because we're challenging the central truth claim of the age, the right to self-autonomy, we should expect fierce opposition. Maintaining our testimony in the face of opposition will take courage.

Daniel knew he hadn't succeeded simply through his great talent or strong work ethic; *God* had prospered him so he could provide courageous testimony in Babylon. Therefore, Daniel leveraged his prosperity to point Babylonians to God, not to himself. He knew he was in Babylon for just a short while to point Babylonians to the God of heaven, and if pointing to that King cost him prosperity . . . well, then, it cost him. As Esther phrased it, "If I perish, I perish." Daniel *expected* to suffer, but he also knew that ultimately he was on the winning side.

We know that even more certainly than Daniel did, because we've seen that Jesus' cross of persecution ended in the victory of resurrection. Just as Shadrach, Meshach, and Abednego went into the fire and came out unharmed, so Jesus went to the cross and emerged from the tomb victorious. We may experience a cross of defeat in the short run, but our story will never end that way. That truth gives us courage.

As Esau McCaulley explains, we must testify to truth and righteousness, "even if it means that we suffer for doing so peacefully," because

> this suffering is only futile if the resurrection is a lie. If the resurrection is true, and the Christian stakes his or her entire existence on its truthfulness, then our peaceful witness testifies to a new and better way of being human that transcends the endless cycle of violence.[8]

The resurrection is what gives us courage. Confidence in the triumph of the resurrection is the secret of our strength in Babylon. To return to the words of Peter,

> Beloved, do not be surprised at the fiery trial when it comes upon you to test you, as though something strange were happening to you. *But rejoice insofar as you share Christ's sufferings, that you may also rejoice and be glad when his glory is revealed.* (1 Peter 4:12–13, emphasis mine)

Don't be surprised when fiery trials come. Expect them. But be just as confident that resurrection is coming, too. As we've shared in Christ's sufferings, we'll also share in his victory.

One Final Caveat

Each generation has its own unique tests of courage. Let's not congratulate ourselves on how bold we can be about things that are no longer controversial.

It takes a lot *less* courage to speak out against overt racism today, for example, than it would have in Charleston, South Carolina, in 1860, and it takes a lot *more* courage to speak up today for the sanctity of life in the womb, God's design for gender, and the exclusivity of Christ for salvation.

An old quote often attributed to Martin Luther goes like this: "The courage of a soldier is tested by how courageously he stands at the place where the battles are the hottest, not how bravely he stands where the battle has passed."[9] We show our courage by our willingness to stand in obedience to God where the culture around us is kneeling *at the moment*. A lot of so-called Christian prophetic speech today amounts to little more than parroting back the world's values and tying Bible verses to them. We show courage by speaking out against those injustices they *don't* acknowledge as sins and celebrate as virtues.

As I said, showing courage will not be easy. Nonetheless, courage is the conduit of God's power in Babylon.

CHAPTER 14

Loud Joy

About midnight Paul and Silas were
praying and singing hymns to God, and
the prisoners were listening to them.
—Acts 16:25

The Christian's business card is joy and
his marketing strategy is love.
—Anonymous

A few years ago our church did a "cardboard testimony" service. If you've never seen one, they work like this: To the backdrop of some worship song, various church members walk across a stage, each holding up a two-by-two-foot piece of cardboard. On one side are a few words describing their lives before Christ, something like this:

"Confused and afraid"
"Anxious, worried, and lonely"
"Never good enough"

After a brief moment they flip their cards over, revealing a brief phrase describing their lives after meeting Jesus:

"Set free"

"Secure and joyful"

"Found real purpose in life"

The best one I've ever seen was a young mom and an older gentleman who walked out onstage together. Her card said, "Diagnosed with MS." The older man then held up his sign, which said, "Doctor who diagnosed her. Atheist." He then flipped his card over, which read, "Baptized this Easter." She then flipped over hers, which said, simply: "Worth it."

But here's the thing: She had not been miraculously healed. To my knowledge, she never got better. It was her joy in suffering, her unquenchable hope, that showed the unbelieving doctor the reality of a God whom he'd been able, up to that point, to ignore.

A miraculous answer to prayer can amaze an unbeliever, and sometimes it leads to their faith. I know of a few stories like that. But quite often—more often than not—the unbeliever who sees the miracle finds a way to explain it away; to convince themselves it was a coincidence, or an exaggeration, or that the doctor misdiagnosed something.

What ends up being *more* convincing to the unbeliever, at least in my observation, is when the believer has an unshakable hope in the midst of tragedy that shows their unbelieving friend something greater, something more permanent than anything a decaying Babylon provides them.

In a cynical, post-Christian world, joy in suffering might be the Christian's most powerful apologetic. It certainly worked that way for Nebuchadnezzar.

"But If Not..."

Nebuchadnezzar threatened to throw Shadrach, Meshach, and Abednego into the fiery furnace for refusing to bow down to his idol. They responded by saying,

"Our God whom we serve is able to deliver us from the burning fiery furnace, and he will deliver us out of your hand, O king. *But if not*, be it known to you, O king, that we will not serve your gods or worship the golden image that you have set up." (Dan. 3:17–18, emphasis added)

Which statement do you think most clearly reveals their faith? Is it

"Our God ... is able to deliver us ... and he will" or
"But if not ... we will not serve your gods"?

The answer, of course, is both, but I'd suggest the words "but if not" were the *most* compelling to Nebuchadnezzar, and I say that because after God had delivered them from the fiery furnace, Nebuchadnezzar said:

"Blessed be the God of Shadrach, Meshach, and Abednego, who ... trusted in him, and set aside the king's command, and *yielded up their bodies rather than serve and worship any god except their own God.*" (Dan. 3:28, emphasis mine)

Nebuchadnezzar talked *more* about Shadrach, Meshach, and Abednego's willingness to die in the flames than he did about God's miraculous deliverance of them! Their willingness to die demonstrated God's reality in ways few other things could. It's awesome when God shows off his miraculous power by answering a prayer in a miraculous way. It's sometimes even more attention grabbing when we show off his inestimable worth by remaining joyful in him even when he doesn't.

I was flipping through the TV channels with my daughter one Saturday morning when I came across one of those televangelists who is always trying to swindle money out of elderly people. This guy was on a roll, and at first I was entertained. He informed us about some big ministry need he had, then promised listeners that if they would give a "seed gift" of at least $1,500, God surely would bless them in response. But then he said something that left my jaw on the floor: "Maybe you think you don't have the money to give. Maybe you can't even pay your bills and have almost maxed out all your credit cards. Well, if there's any room left on that card, I want to urge you to fill up whatever room is left by giving to this ministry. If you do that, God will reward your faith by cutting your debts in half, and when God has paid off your credit cards, and you are driving that new BMW, everyone will see that smile on your face and be amazed at the miraculous things God has done in your life."

I don't think Christians should make a habit of cussing, but if ever there were a time I felt it might be justified, it was this moment. The thought of this man swindling lonely older people out of their life savings made me want to fly to his city and punch him in the throat. I know that's not the right reaction, but it's how I felt. Apart from the shameless greed behind the whole charade, what he said also struck me as illogical. *Why would your neighbors be amazed to see a smile on your face as you drove a new BMW?* Wouldn't *anyone* smile in that circumstance?

It's when everything in your life goes wrong and that smile stays on your face that the world pays attention.

I'm not trying to say God never brings glory to himself through miraculous provision. I'm saying that what gets a cynical world's attention the quickest is when a Christian possesses unshakable joy even when everything goes wrong. That alerts them to the reality of another, even more real, even more important world than the Babylon they see in front of them.

John Newton, the writer of the song "Amazing Grace," had formerly served as captain of a slave ship. After a radical conversion he not only repented of his ways but locked arms with William

Wilberforce to shut down the slave trade in the Western world. Newton's conversion cost him dearly. Initially he lost income, friends, and his stature in society. People asked him how he remained joyful through it all. He told them he was like a man who had been told that he was inheriting an estate worth millions of dollars, and when on his way to claim it his carriage broke down. Rather than bemoaning his poor luck, however, this man would leave the dilapidated carriage behind and joyfully skip the rest of the way to the bank to claim his fortune. "What a fool we would think that man," Newton said, "if we saw him wringing his hands, and blubbering out through tears for the remaining mile, 'Oh no, my carriage is broken! My carriage is broken!' He'd be a fool because just up ahead is a greater fortune than he could possibly imagine."[1]

It's when we bounce with joy down the road of life, with all its problems, sure of the glorious inheritance we have waiting for us that Nebuchadnezzar begins to understand the reality and the value of the heavenly realm.

So, by all means, pray for healing and provision, and give God glory for it when it comes. But when God chooses not to answer the prayer the way you want, realize you have an even greater opportunity to let him shine. The path may be painful, but from the perspective of eternity, when you flip over the card of your life, it will surely say "Worth it."

I've heard it said: Sometimes God is glorified when sick Christians *get* well; other times he is glorified when sick Christians *die* well.

I'm not saying you shouldn't pray for relief from sickness, suffering, or financial ruin. Suffering is a bitter road and one I'd never intentionally choose. I'm saying that when God leads you down that road, receive it as part of his plan and leverage it as the gospel opportunity that it is. Life is short, and eternity is forever. All of this life's misfortunes are, to use Paul's words, "light" and "momentary" (2 Cor. 4:17).

A Joy That Cuts Through the Noise

Ironically enough, it was joy in suffering that Luke identified as a primary factor in the establishment of the first church in Europe.

In Acts 16 Luke recounted Paul's missionary foray into Philippi. Philippi was a cosmopolitan Roman city in Europe with very little Jewish presence and no Christian one. Luke organized his story of the founding of the church there around the conversion of three different Philippians, and how they come to Christ establishes a pattern for ministry work in purple cities.

The first convert Luke wrote about is Lydia, a well-to-do, put-together religious businesswoman. She was already spiritually interested, a "worshiper of God" (Acts 16:14). She came to Christ through one of Paul's "seeker" Bible studies (vv. 13–15).

The second convert was on the opposite end of the spectrum: a poor slave girl, oppressed and demon possessed. Bringing her to Christ meant first casting the demon out of her, delivering her from her spiritual and economic bondage (vv. 16–18). She never would have been reached by one of Paul's investigative Bible studies. To reach her, Paul had to get involved in her suffering.

The third convert in Philippi was a Roman jailer. Jailers in those days were usually retired soldiers who were given a jail to run as a reward for their service. Battle scarred and war weary, they were usually pretty cynical. How did this cynical jailer come to Christ? *By observing Paul and Silas's joy in the midst of suffering* (vv. 25–34).

After being beaten and locked up in the inner prison dungeon, Paul and Silas responded by singing psalms of thanksgiving and joy. Luke tells us "the prisoners were listening" (v. 25), and as we will see, the jailer was listening, too. Later that night, God sent an earthquake that knocked the prison walls down and the prisoners' chains off. Instead of taking his chance to escape, however, Paul turned back to the jailer and said, "Do not harm yourself, for we are all still here." You see, Roman law said that a jailer who lost his prisoners for any reason would pay with his life, so when the jailer had seen that his prisoners were free, he'd drawn his sword to take his own life so he could spare himself and his family the humiliation of a public trial.

The jailer was so moved by their joy and compassion that he fell to his knees and said, "Sirs, what must I do to be saved?" (v. 30). The jailer seemed more shaken by Paul and Silas's joy and kindness than he had been by the earthquake!

I believe Luke intended the profile of these converts to be a kind of grid for how we can expect to reach the different populations in our Babylon:

- Think of "Lydias" as spiritually interested people who will be reached through evangelistic events such as seeker-oriented Bible studies and Easter services.
- Think of "slave girls" as those physical, economic, or spiritual captives who likely can't, or won't, come to our Bible studies. We must meet them where they are, working to deliver them from their bondage.
- Think of the "jailers" as cynics in government, education, or the arts. They will be won as we demonstrate unflagging joy and extraordinary generosity in persecution.[2]

I've often wondered: Why didn't Paul see the earthquake as God's miraculous provision for setting him free? Just a few chapters prior, Peter was set free from prison when an angel opened Peter's prison door (Acts 12:5–19). Wasn't God doing the same thing for Paul through this earthquake?

Paul perceived that God was doing something bigger and better than merely setting him free. God hadn't sent Paul to Philippi just to stay out of jail but to testify to a city full of captives that God could set them free, too. The best way Paul could testify to that was by staying in captivity for a few hours and focusing on the soul of the Philippian jailer. Paul won the jailer not through philosophical argumentation but through joy and generosity.

Joy in the midst of suffering and persecution speaks with a clarity and at a volume that sometimes even our sermons cannot. Joy in suffering screams *hope*, a hope that drives citizens of Babylon to ask, "Where does that joy come from? I want that!" (see 1 Peter 3:15).

As Tim Keller observes,

> Christians should be experts in joy . . . but we're not. And that's because we focus on the pleasures and blessings instead of the Blesser.[3]

Joy in suffering puts the pleasurability of *God himself* on display. If you're going to strive to be an expert at anything in Babylon, ask God to make you an expert in joy! That way, when you walk through the fire, they'll see Jesus walking with you and will be amazed at the joy and peace emanating from your face as you pass through those flames. They won't see the singe of cynicism on your hair or smell the scent of despair on your clothes. What they'll see is the kind of freedom and joy they crave from the bottom of their hearts.

And they'll glorify your Father in heaven.

Suffering is an opportunity. You don't have to enjoy it, but don't waste it. It's one of the loudest megaphones you have in Babylon.

CHAPTER | 15

Loud Generosity

Let your light shine before others, so that
they may see your good works and give
glory to your Father who is in heaven.
—MATTHEW 5:16

My favorite movie scene of all time is in the opening sequence of the 1998 rendition of Victor Hugo's *Les Misérables*. Jean Valjean, played by Liam Neeson, is a bitter criminal, newly paroled from a hard-labor camp where he has served twenty years for stealing a loaf of bread. No one will hire him or give him shelter. Filled with anger, self-pity, and bitterness, he stumbles to a priest's home. The pastor opens his door and invites Jean Valjean to eat at his table.

Valjean repays the priest's hospitality by physically assaulting him and stealing all his silverware. The next morning Valjean is stopped by the police, who discover the stolen silver and drag him back to the priest's home. If the priest confirms that Valjean stole the silverware, Valjean will go back to prison for life. The incensed guard exclaims to the priest, "And this man had the audacity to claim you *gave* the silver to him!"

The priest, his face still bruised from being struck by Valjean the night before, looks into Valjean's eyes and says, "I'm very angry with you, Jean Valjean." But then, unexpectedly, he continues,

"Because you forgot the candlesticks. Why did you forget the candlesticks? They are worth more than two thousand francs." He shoves the candlesticks into his bag and tells Valjean he must be on his way.

The guard, flabbergasted, says, "You know this man? You gave him this silver? He didn't steal it?" The priest, now looking directly into Valjean's eyes, nods his head, and the guard orders Valjean to be released. The priest then grabs Valjean by the shoulders, leans up closely toward his face, and says, "Don't you forget. Don't you ever forget. You've promised to become a new man! Jean Valjean, my brother, you no longer belong to evil. With this silver I've bought your soul. I've ransomed you from fear and hatred, and now I give you back to God."

Les Misérables recounts the story of how Jean Valjean becomes the "new man" the priest commanded he become. One act of unexpected, undeserved kindness transformed Valjean from a bitter criminal into an extravagantly kind, generous man who cared for the poor and literally laid down his life for the widow and the orphan.

Victor Hugo's inspiration for that account, of course, was the gospel story itself, and Hugo aimed to communicate one undeniable truth:

Those who have been the recipients of great grace become great distributors of it to others.

A Generosity That Preaches

In their letters to the church, both Peter and Paul explained that the extravagance of gospel-inspired generosity will be one of the primary ways that a hostile, unbelieving world will come to recognize that something truly *divine* is going on inside us. Our generosity of spirit, our penchant for forgiveness, and the depth of our compassion lead others to ask *the reason* for the hope that drives us.

As we saw in the previous chapter, it was the extravagance of Paul's generosity that, in part, drove the cynical Roman jailer to fall trembling at his feet to inquire how he, too, might be saved. Seeing Paul turn his back on his own rightful chance at freedom so that he could rescue him opened his heart to Paul's gospel.

The church historian Rodney Stark says it was the extraordinary generosity of the early church that made Christianity indomitable in an empire intent on crushing it. Stark explains that this generosity of spirit manifested itself in three primary ways:

> First, early Christians did not flee sickness when plague ravaged Rome. When most everyone else fled the cities, Christians stayed, ministering to the sick. They reasoned that because Jesus was a healer who had risen from the dead, they, too, should stay and bring healing to the sick.
>
> Second, early Christians forgave those who persecuted them. Many groups were persecuted by Rome, but Christians did not form vigilante groups to fight back. They forgave their captors, reasoning that if Jesus' greatest victory had come through persecution, theirs would, too.
>
> Third, early Christian churches were one of the only places in the Roman Empire where socially and ethnically divided groups lived together in unity. The Roman Empire had forced disparate populations to live together in vast metroplexes for one of the first times in human history, and the resulting cultural strife was intense. Christians reasoned that if Christ was the Lord of all humanity, however, then all people were equally valuable before him, more alike than they were different. As Jesus had reconciled warring humanity to God by absorbing the conflict

into himself, his followers could do the same with their historical enemies.[1]

(By the way, let's revisit Paul in Philippi for a second because this is too good to pass up! According to the Siddur [the first-century Jewish prayer book], every morning Jewish men would thank God each morning that they were not "a woman, a slave, or a Gentile." The first church service in Philippi would have included a woman, a slave, a Gentile, and a Jewish rabbi!)

Each of these behaviors, we see, was a direct response to the gospel. These generous behaviors accentuated their preaching, making it irresistible. They compelled the community to ask, "Why are you Christians the way that you are?"

Even Christianity's critics were forced to acknowledge that their generosity pointed to something extraordinary. The fourth-century Roman emperor Julian, for example, known as Julian the Apostate, groused in a famous letter to his friend Arsacius, the pagan high priest of Galatia, that he could not stop the growth of the church no matter how hard he tried. He complained,

Atheism [by this he means the Christian faith!] has been specially advanced through the loving service rendered to strangers, and through their care for the burial of the dead. It is a scandal that there is not a single Jew who is a beggar, and that the godless Galileans care not only for their own poor but for ours as well; while those who belong to us look in vain for the help that we should render them.[2]

Historian Eberhard Arnold notes, "Most astounding to the outside observer was the extent to which poverty was overcome in the vicinity of the communities, through voluntary works of love. . . . Christians spent more money in the streets than the followers of other religions spent in their temples."³ Missionary Lesslie Newbigin observed that evangelism in the book of Acts is essentially a group of people coming together to ask the church, "What is going on among you people?"

Recently I heard that a local church in Tennessee paid off the medical debts of nearly four thousand people in their community.⁴ It's hard for that kind of generosity to go unnoticed, and hard for the community not to ask what would motivate a church to sacrifice like that. As Francis Schaeffer once said, love on display in the Christian community is Jesus' "final apologetic."⁵

Uniquely Christian

Generosity is not unique to Christianity, of course, but there is something distinct about both the *nature* and the *extent* of Christian generosity. It arises in the most unlikely of places to the most extravagant of degrees. As we saw in a previous chapter, it seeks nothing in return, pouring out its favors on those who cannot pay it back.

Uniquely Christian generosity mimics the sacrifice Jesus made for us. Others perceive in our actions the beauty of some scene precious to us that we long to re-create, the echo of a tune we want to hear played again. Paul turned his back on his freedom to go back for the Roman jailer *because* he knew Jesus had turned his back on freedom to come after him. Later, urging the Corinthians to be generous, Paul implored them to remember "the grace of our Lord Jesus Christ, that though he was rich, yet for your sake he became poor, so that you by his poverty might become rich" (2 Cor. 8:9).

When Stephen, the first Christian martyr, was having his life pummeled out of him by the rocks the members of the Sanhedrin were throwing at him, he called out two final phrases:

"Lord Jesus, receive my spirit. . . . Lord, do not hold this sin against them." (Acts 7:59–60)

Several in the audience that day recognized these two phrases, because they were nearly identical to what Jesus had prayed when he died:

"Father, into your hands I commit my spirit! . . . Father, forgive them, for they know not what they do." (Luke 23:46, 34)

It seems that in Stephen's dying moments he was thinking about what Jesus had prayed on the cross for him, and he was now praying those very things for others. He was attempting to do for others what Jesus had done for him. Because, you see, that's what it means to follow Jesus: to do for others what Jesus did for you.

It has been said that those who believe the gospel inevitably become like the gospel. They can't help it! As with Jean Valjean, there's simply no way to experience the extraordinary generosity of the gospel and not become extraordinarily generous yourself. It becomes a tune you must play, an instinct you can't ignore. It's more than just a general disposition to "niceness"—it's a taste for radical generosity that periodically breaks into your own behavior.

It's what Christopher Hitchens saw in Larry Taunton, and what the young woman our pastor met in the airport got a small taste of when he paid for the bagels of the mom struggling to keep her kids under control. Babylonians don't always embrace (or even approve of) our beliefs, but they see something in us that is good, pure, and beautiful. And it attracts them.

Our compassion, while not showy, grabs attention. It shines like a star in a dark sky, like a harbinger of an otherworldly kingdom on its way to earth. It's what Romans noticed about the early Christians. It's what the community in Tennessee sensed when that church paid off its medical debts. It's what that university professor I told you about at the beginning of this book saw in our church's work with the poor.

It's the boss who takes the blame for the mistake of one of his interns. Or the manager who shows up to care for the employee who tried to get him fired. It's Stephen praying for those persecuting him and Paul turning his back on his freedom to go back for the jailer. It's your church taking care of the widow and orphan in your community or the myriad others who can never really repay your kindness. It's showing grace to those who are trying to hurt you.

Gospel-fueled grace confuses and bewilders our community and drives them to ask the reason for the hope that is within us.

Gospel-Fed, Spirit-Led

But how do you know *when* to show this radical kind of generosity? After all, the Jesus-imitating boss doesn't necessarily take the fall for *every* mistake his or her employee makes. The priest in *Les Misérables* didn't offer his candlesticks to every paroled prisoner who passed through town.

There's not a simple answer—we Christians have a general disposition toward acts of grace and mercy, and the apostles instruct us to do good to all wherever we can (Gal. 6:10; James 4:17). But when do you do something *radical*?

The short answer is that the Holy Spirit must guide you. As Jesus explained, ministry is not something we do for God but something we do *with* him—that is, in concert with his Spirit. Even Jesus saw his ministry as joining the Father in what *the Father* was doing (John 5:17–19). Jesus didn't heal every sick person in Israel; he healed only the ones the Father led him to.

Christians listen for the prompting of the Holy Spirit to know when and where we are to demonstrate the radical grace of the gospel. When we read Acts, we don't see a group of accomplished

Christian leaders going out to attempt great things for God as much as we see a group of unqualified followers trying to keep up with him as he "acted" around them. The Holy Spirit was the real mover, the real "Act-er," in the book of Acts. He shows up fifty-nine times in the book of Acts, and in thirty-six of the fifty-nine he is instructing members of the church where and how to show off God's power.

That's still true today. The Holy Spirit is the Act-er, guiding us where and how to put his radical generosity on display.

The Worst Christian of 2019

One afternoon a package showed up at my church office with no return address on it. I opened it up to find a moderately sized trophy with a golden calf sitting on top bearing the inscription, "Worst Christian of 2019: J. D. Greear, Pastor of the Summit Church, President of the Southern Baptist Convention."

At first I thought one of our other church staff had sent it to me as a joke, but when I searched "Worst Christian of 2019," I discovered that a few popular blogger-podcasters (whom I had never met) had hosted an online contest to determine who, in their audience's opinion, were the "worst" Christians that year. Their criteria, they explained, were those Christians whom God had put into positions of influence who had used them most deleteriously. Specifically, they were upset about some things I had said about the church's failure to properly protect victims of sexual abuse and racial injustice and to stand up to hate crimes against gay people. They thought it was too much of a compromise with the "woke mob," leading conservative churches down paths of compromise. For that reason they awarded me the dishonorific "Worst Christian of 2019."

I try not to let stuff like that bother me—I know it goes with the territory. Yet I'd be lying if I said that their mockery didn't bother me a little. This blog-podcast community occupies only a small corner of the Christian world, but still. Nobody likes to have their motives impugned or their name trashed like that.

About a year and a half later, however, one of the primary blogger-podcasters behind a lot of the criticism directed at me got arrested for drunk driving and opioid abuse. I heard about it, and there was a small part of me that wanted to say, "Well, serves him right. He dug a pit and fell into it himself, just like Proverbs says." But then the Holy Spirit overwhelmed me with thoughts about his wife and kids, and the church he helps lead, and how devastating this must have been for all of them. And the Spirit of God reminded me how many times I'd lashed out in anger toward someone when I didn't know all the facts, just as he had done with me.

The Holy Spirit then impressed upon me exactly what he wanted me to do—to write and tell him I was praying for him and that God had a second chance for him. I knew he may not be too keen on hearing from me, of course. So I found out where he lived and bought him and his wife a gift card to the nicest restaurant I could find in his area and jotted him a note that said something like "Thank God we serve a Savior of second chances who thrives in helping us rebuild our lives after mistakes. Praying for you and your family right now and believing God will be with you for what he has ahead for you."

I never expected to hear back from him. About a year later, however, someone pointed me to a podcast he'd recently been on. He had just gotten out of rehab, and apparently this was his first public appearance since the scandal had broken.

Just looking at him on this podcast, I knew something was different. He spoke with humility. He explained how many of his so-called friends—friends who joined him in trashing other Christians, friends he thought had cared about him—had treated him as though he had a disease when his addiction and arrest became public. He had become a liability to them, and they seemed to want nothing to do with him.

"But meanwhile," he said, "do you know who I was hearing from? Beth Moore[6] and J. D. Greear. These people were sending me gift cards to my house and telling me they are praying for me. At first I thought they were just spiking the ball in my face. But it became evident that they were doing this because they genuinely cared."[7]

I don't know what the future is for this guy, and I'm not claiming a relatively small gift card made any real difference. But it did get his attention more than any of my well-reasoned defenses had. The point is that God reveals his gospel to a hostile world through grace and generosity of spirit.

Paul explained this in his letter to the Romans. Grace, not retribution, transforms those who persecute, he said. I love how *The Message* renders this his words:

> Bless your enemies; no cursing under your breath. . . . Get along with each other; don't be stuck-up. Make friends with nobodies; don't be the great somebody.
>
> Don't hit back; discover beauty in everyone. If you've got it in you, get along with everybody. Don't insist on getting even; that's not for you to do. "I'll do the judging," says God. "I'll take care of it."
>
> Our Scriptures tell us that if you see your enemy hungry, go buy that person lunch, or if he's thirsty, get him a drink. Your generosity will surprise him with goodness. Don't let evil get the best of you; get the best of evil by doing good. (12:14–21 MSG)

When you live with that kind of generosity of spirit, you're showing something that words alone are incapable of showing. Through your actions, Babylon gets a glimpse of a King far superior to Nebuchadnezzar, even with his massive armies and hanging gardens.

So don't be discouraged when others treat you unfairly. Peter said these are opportunities to put the distinctiveness of that King on display—which is why we are here. Remember:

You were called to this, because Christ also suffered for you,
leaving you an example, that you should follow in his steps.
(1 Peter 2:21 CSB)

Let that sink in:

You were called to this.

When you suffer, it's not that you've done something wrong. It's
not that God forgot about you. It's not even that God begrudgingly
allowed your suffering. No, you suffer because *that's what you were
called to.* And your response of generosity—with your money, your
time, your forgiveness—is how God puts the *distinctive* beauty of his
kingdom on display.

Suffering is not the accidental byproduct of gospel ministry, or
what happens when you don't properly contextualize your message.
Suffering is what happens when you live as Jesus did. You were *called*
to this. Generosity in suffering screams so loudly that even a world
trying to close its ears has to listen.

No Strings Attached?

One of our most vibrant ministries at the Summit Church is our
outreach to prisoners. Over the years we've started weekly Sunday
gatherings in nine different prison facilities in the area, and we've
seen hundreds of incarcerated men and women profess faith in
Christ. (There have been 166 professions of faith there in the past two
years alone!)

Recently a couple of our church members felt burdened over how
difficult it was for many of these prisoners to reintegrate into the real
world upon their release, so they started a ministry called Restorative

Transitions that seeks to provide affordable housing, job training, and ongoing discipleship for newly released prisoners.

One of the ministry leaders explained that she often gets skeptical questions from prisoners, especially those who aren't Christians yet, about why we do all of this. One kept pressing her, "So when does the 'ask' come? Surely," he said, "nobody does all of this for free with no strings attached."

The ministry leader explained that we don't do this because of something we hope to get from you in the future but because of something done for us in the past. Our lives have been shaped forever by Jesus' kindness shown to us, and now we can't help but show that same kindness to others.

As Jesus explained after teaching on the good Samaritan,

Go, and do thou likewise. (Luke 10:37 KJV)

CHAPTER | 16

Loud Hospitality

Do not neglect to show hospitality to strangers.
—HEBREWS 13:2

If I had to come up with a list of people least likely to become a Christian, Rosaria Butterfield would be at the top of that list.

Rosaria was a liberal professor of English and women's studies at Syracuse University and a practicing lesbian and outspoken feminist. She specialized in queer theory, publishing numerous articles and books on the subject. She was a sought-after speaker around the country, advocating for gay pride at universities as prestigious as Harvard. She even drafted and lobbied for Syracuse's first successful domestic-partnership policy, giving spousal benefits to homosexual couples.

In the late 1990s she picked a fight with a Christian movement called Promise Keepers, a movement that emphasized the need for Christian men to step forward in their leadership roles as husbands and fathers. Pretty much the polar opposite of her life's work.

She wrote a blistering piece in her city newspaper about the harmfulness of the movement, and, as you might imagine, she got all kinds of responses. No neutral ones, of course—they were filled with either fawning praise or damning invectives. For a while, she said, she kept two empty printer boxes on her desk for the responses: "You're awesome" notes in one box, and "I hate you, you spawn of the devil" notes in the other.

One afternoon, however, she opened up a letter from a local pastor named Ken Smith. It was clear he strongly disagreed with her, but his letter was so full of kindness and respect, so "kind and inquiring," that she genuinely didn't know what pile it belonged in.[1]

At first she threw it away. But she couldn't stop thinking about it. So she pulled it out of the trash, left it on her desk, and just stared at it for a few days. Eventually she called up the pastor and asked whether she could ask him some questions (purely for her research, of course), and he invited her to his house for dinner with his family. Her lesbian partner didn't understand why she was going. She showed up ready for debate, but what overwhelmed her about this pastor and his wife was their gracious hospitality. There were so many people coming to their house, she said, it was as if the front door didn't actually exist.[2]

She became a regular guest there, and, to make a long story short, through their love and patient guidance in the Scriptures, she eventually came to faith in Christ. She now lives just a few miles from me. She is a pastor's wife and a mother of four children, two of whom are foster adoptions. We've gotten together several times, and I consider her a friend.

She wrote a book a few years ago called *The Gospel Comes with a House Key* in which she makes the case, using herself as an example, that in today's climate, hospitality is the primary way people outside the church will be reached. Many secular people have no interest, she says, in hearing an evangelistic presentation, no matter how compellingly it's presented. The truth is, they see our eloquent confidence as part of the problem!

How do we make space for God talk in such an emotionally charged atmosphere? she asks.

The same way Jesus did: by sitting around tables eating and drinking together.

Hospitality was the tip of Jesus' outreach spear. As Robert Karris notes, Jesus ate his way through the gospel of Luke! The whole narrative of Luke is organized around meals.[3]

Honestly, y'all, that's my kind of Savior.

The British pastor Tim Chester, in a great little book called *A Meal with Jesus*,[4] points out that Luke used the phrase "The Son of Man came . . ." to describe Jesus' ministry twice. Luke 19:10 says,

"The Son of Man came to seek and to save the lost."

We're familiar with that one. But earlier, in Luke 7:34, he said,

"The Son of Man has come eating and drinking."

As John Mark Comer notes, Luke 19:10 gives us Jesus' *mission*, seeking and saving the lost. Luke 7:34 gives us his *method*: eating and drinking.[5] One scholar even said, "Jesus got himself crucified by the *way* that he ate."[6]

In a sometimes hostile culture, where we live as spiritual strangers and exiles, our homes are often the most valuable tools we have for engaging others with the gospel. Our witness, Butterfield says, is supposed to include an open invitation—a "house key"—to our lives:

> Those who live out radically ordinary hospitality see their homes not as theirs at all but as God's gift to use for the furtherance of his kingdom. . . . My prayer is that this book will help you let God use your home, apartment, dorm room, front yard, community gymnasium, or garden for the purpose of making strangers into neighbors and neighbors into family.

She suggests that the bedrock for effective gospel ministry is laid simply by being a good neighbor. A few years ago, my family and I had dinner with her at her house, and over dinner she told me: "The only social media I am on is the Nextdoor app. I am the Nextdoor queen! I know when anything happens with my neighbors, and I am the first one there offering help."

For whatever it's worth, over the years I've recommended *lots* of books on evangelism to our church. By far the most popular has been Rosaria's *The Gospel Comes with a Housekey*. People come back to it again and again. I think what makes it so compelling is that she shows us that outreach is something all of us can do. We each eat around 1,095 meals every year; outreach means opening up 20 or 30 of them to Babylonians. As my friend John Mark Comer says, "I may not be able to solve the great systemic injustices of our time, but I can cook some of the best pizza you've ever had."[7] As they eat your pizza, you can model for them the warmth of the kingdom and, most, certainly, opportunities will arise for you to testify to them about your hope in Jesus.

Rosaria says, "Stop thinking of witnessing to your neighbors as sneaky evangelistic raids into their sinful lives." Instead, open up your lives to them and share with them the warmth of your home. "For words to be persuasive," she says, "they can't be stronger than relationships."[8]

Hospitality might be the great lost art of Christianity. Most of us can't even define it correctly anymore (I'll show you that in a minute)! Yet excellence in hospitality was considered so central to apostolic ministry that Paul made it one of the *requirements* for a church leader. Elders should be "given to hospitality" (1 Tim. 3:2 KJV). "Given to" means that you have a passion for it and do it all the time.

With the help of Butterfield and a few others, let me suggest four reasons *why* gospel hospitality has been lost in our generation, and how we can recover it as part of our witness in Babylon.

Obstacle 1: We Have the Wrong Definition of Hospitality

Today when most Christians think about hospitality, they think about entertaining church friends in their homes. Biblically that's called *fellowship*, and it's important, too. In biblical parlance, however, hospitality means welcoming in *the stranger*. The foreigner. The non-Christian.

In her book *Making Room*, Christine Pohl writes: "One of the key Greek words for hospitality, *philoxenia*, combines the general word for love or affection for people who are connected to us by kinship or faith (*phileo*), and the word for stranger (*xenos*)."[9] Hospitality is showing family-like love to the outsider.

Hospitality demonstrates a crucial distinctive quality of our King Jesus: his love for outsiders and his yearning to bring them in. He came not just to fellowship with the righteous but to seek and save the lost.

This is so central to the heart of Jesus that he considers our welcoming in of the stranger to be an act of kindness toward him *personally*. He said in the gospel of Matthew:

> "Then the King will say to those on his right, 'Come, you who are blessed by my Father, inherit the kingdom prepared for you from the foundation of the world. For I was hungry and you gave me food, I was thirsty and you gave me drink, *I was a stranger and you welcomed me. . . .* Truly, I say to you, as you did it to one of the least of these my brothers, you did it to me.'" (Matt. 25:34–35, 40, emphasis mine)

Jesus specifically had in view marginalized, persecuted *believers* in this passage, but what he said was consistent with how he said we are to treat *all* the poor. In Proverbs 19:17 King Solomon said, "Whoever is generous to the poor *lends to the LORD*" (emphasis mine). *When you gave to the poor or welcomed in the stranger*, Jesus said, *you welcomed me*.[10]

"Fellowship" is important, too, of course. There is simply no way to fulfill all the "one another" instructions given to the church in the New Testament unless we believers are *regularly* sitting around one another's tables, too. But followers of Jesus should not limit their guest lists to family and Christian friends.

So ask yourself: When was the last time someone sat around my dinner table that didn't really "belong" there, in the "family, friend, and tribe" sense?

Does the single mom ever sit around your table?

The orphan?

The liberal neighbor?

Do you ever share a meal with the elderly or the invalid?

Do you ever break bread with a newly released prisoner?

Jesus said that for his followers the "party" of their lives should be thrown for those who can't pay them back. The first and most literal place to apply that instruction is around our dinner tables!

Obstacle 2: We Are Afraid

Many of us, Butterfield explains, view our houses as our "safe castles." As such, we want only safe, enjoyable, value-adding people in them.

That's not, however, how Jesus called his followers to view their homes. The homes Jesus visited in the Gospels became theaters for God's glory, hospital waiting rooms where sick patients met the Healer. They were not just safe castles; they were battlefronts.

Hospitality, Butterfield explains, is often inconvenient, and sometimes it exposes our families to messy Babylonian stuff. The greater danger, she says, is not what some stranger may introduce to our family but what happens in our hearts (and our kids' hearts) when we live sheltered, self-centered lives.[11]

Lance Ford explains in his book *Next Door as It Is in Heaven* that it was fear that kept his family from getting involved in foster care. He came to realize, however, that the greater danger to his family was not what foster kids would bring into his kids' lives but the risk of his own kids growing up disconnected from the mission of Jesus. He says,

> When talking about foster care, I will often share 3 benefits of providing care: First, it is a wonderful way to influence the lives of hurting children. Second, in many cases there is a great opportunity to influence the lives of the parent or parents, who in most circumstances is a single mother. But third, providing care for these children is the single best thing we have ever done for our own kids. We have learned how God uses hospitality to shape and form us. That is a fascinating aspect of kingdom living. As you bestow a blessing for the benefit of others, you realize that you too are a recipient of God's grace.[12]

As we often say at the Summit Church, the best way to improve your own relationship with Jesus is to help somebody else with theirs. Ford and his coauthor, Brad Brisco, then observe, quite poignantly,

> The real question is not, "How dangerous is that stranger?" The real question is, "How dangerous will I become if I am not more open?"[13]

"Stranger danger" is not the real danger to our families—being *disconnected* from the stranger is. Because in welcoming the stranger, we find Jesus.

Growing in Christlikeness is so much more than cleaning up your language, memorizing some verses, and getting busy in church. As David Platt says, God didn't save you to sanitize you and put you on the shelf; he saved you to send you into service![14] Jesus converted us not to quarantine us but to commission us! In service is where the real adventure lies.

And you never know what you'll get to experience in a life devoted to service. It's so much more fun than trying to live a nice, safe life. A couple of my best friends began to serve our local refugee community. One of them, Ashley, told us that at first fear paralyzed her from really getting involved. Her family became acquainted with an Afghan Muslim family who spoke almost no English. She asked the Afghan man what he most needed, and the man said, "Pressure cooker." She was having a little trouble understanding what he was saying, and he said, "Do you know what pressure cooker is? Very powerful. Like bomb. Cooks fast."

"All I could think about," she said, "was 'pressure cooker' and 'bomb' and how I'd heard from the agency that this man might have formerly been connected to the Taliban in Afghanistan. Eventually my husband and I bought them a *slow* cooker and took it over to their house. A slow cooker is similar to a pressure cooker but takes about eight hours longer. I figured if he did have ill intent, that would at least slow him down." After a while she saw that all he wanted was to cook rice for a traditional meal for his homesick kids. "Being engaged in this community has brought us lots of adventures, but the richness these relationships have brought into my family, I wouldn't trade for anything.... The day they moved, the Afghani's wife told me, in very broken English, that she dreamed that Jesus came to her to tell her he was her friend. She cried, hugged me, and told me she is now friends with Jesus."

Leading people to friendship with Jesus starts with friendship with us, and that usually happens around our tables.

I'm not telling you to throw all caution to the wind, of course—Jesus, after all, tells us to be wise as serpents and harmless as doves. I'm saying that growth in Christlikeness means taking these kinds of risks and opening up your life to the outsider. This is part of what it means to live as a kingdom representative in Babylon. Under the leadership of the Spirit, you can open up your home to a Jean Valjean and show him incredible grace around your table.

Obstacle 3: We View Hospitality as Performance Rather Than Service

Many of us struggle to apply hospitality because we see it as some kind of performance we're being evaluated on. We feel pressure to make guests assume we eat five-star meals every night and live in a pristine, perfectly appointed setting worthy of *Better Homes and Gardens*. Thus, we're intimidated to open up our *actual* homes because of what others will think about us, and we think somehow we've been rude to them if we don't deliver Michelin-rating-worthy white-glove treatment.

Butterfield says true hospitality means opening up your *normal* life to those on the outside, not auditioning for *Ballard Designs*. She calls it "radically ordinary hospitality." The assumption that everything must be perfect, she says, keeps many Christians from opening up their homes as the apostles commanded:

> We sometimes forget that the Christian life is a calling, not a performance. Hospitality is necessary whether you have cat hair on the couch or not. People will die of chronic loneliness sooner than they will cat hair in the soup.[15]

Maybe you should consider getting rid of the cat. Nothing good comes from the cat world, and in the New Testament when Peter chose an animal to depict Satan, he chose a member of the cat family (1 Peter 5:8). I'm just saying. (Just a joke!) But the point is not to let pride over how clean your house is keep you from using it for the kingdom. Your identity is not in a perfect home, it's in being a servant of Jesus. Our homes are auditoriums for Jesus' teaching, theaters for his glory, and waiting rooms in his hospital, not photo sets for *House Beautiful* magazine.

Our mission is too important to let what others think about our housekeeping skills paralyze us. My wife often says that what others most need to see from us anyway is the *real* us, not some filtered, airbrushed version of us. The fake version of us can't help them. But seeing that Jesus loves and fellowships with us in the midst of our mess, she says, just might open their hearts to see that he can minister to them in theirs.

Obstacle 4: We Lack Margin

Finally, the biggest challenge to showing this kind of hospitality is the lack of margin that characterizes our hyperscheduled, overly busy lives. Butterfield says,

> Practicing radically ordinary hospitality necessitates building margin time into the day, time where regular routines can be disrupted but not destroyed. This margin stays open for the Lord to fill—to take an older neighbor to the doctor, to babysit on the fly, to make room for a family displaced by a flood or a worldwide refugee crisis. Living out radically ordinary hospitality leaves us with plenty to share, because we intentionally live below our means.[16]

Ford and Brisco concur. Without margin, they say, we will be incapable of investing in our neighbors in the spontaneous way that relationships require. Without margin we won't have the space to meet their needs. Margin gives us the ability to be *interruptible* for God's purposes, an interruptibility essential for good hospitality.[17]

One of my favorite college history professors taught for several years at West Point. One of his favorite military-history life lessons was "War is won by reserves." By that he meant that generals who prevailed in battle often did so because they kept reserve troops and supplies in waiting, so that when a moment of opportunity appeared on the battlefield, they could take advantage of it. Effective Christian ministry is done by those with time and money reserves—those with just enough time reserved in their days and just enough money set aside in their budgets that they can meet hospitality opportunities when God presents them.

You Can Do It ... In Fact, You're *Already* Doing It!

John Mark Comer says that the beauty of this method of evangelism is that not only is it (a) something any follower of Jesus can do, but it's (b) something you are already doing. After all, you're eating regularly. Jeff Vanderstelt, a pastor in Seattle, says that evangelism and discipleship in a post-Christian context is simply "doing normal life with gospel intentionality."[18]

I can say without any hesitation that it doesn't matter who you are, how long you've been a Christian, or what your spiritual gifts are: This is part of God's plan for your life. Every Christian can practice hospitality, and every Christian leader, as Paul said, should excel at it.

Remember Jesus' final words to his disciples before he ascended: "You will be my *witnesses* in Jerusalem and in all Judea and Samaria, and to the end of the earth" (Acts 1:8, emphasis mine). Think of all the labels Jesus could have given them there! He could have said, "And you will be my ... *Bible studiers.*" Or "You will be my *pray-ers* ... my *worship-song singers* ... my *justice advocates.*" Any of these things would have been true. What he said, however, was "You will be my *witnesses.*"

As we've seen, that means whatever else we do in life, our primary role is to witness to Jesus.

Gospel hospitality is how most of us *best* apply that.

214

Maybe you've always found "evangelism" intimidating. You think you don't have the right personality for it; you're not a trained theologian or don't think well on your feet, or you're not sure where to start.

Start with what you're *already* doing—eating three times a day, going to the gym, sitting on your back porch watching a football game. What if being a witness simply means opening up these parts of your life to people on the outside, letting them see how you think, how you talk, how you pray, how you process joy, disappointment, and pain? And in those moments when the Holy Spirit opens a door for you to share the reason for the hope that motivates and shapes you, take it. Ninety percent of evangelism is being in the right place at the right time so that you can, under the leadership of the Spirit, point to Jesus.

Hospitality puts you in those right places.

So why not invite someone over tomorrow night?

We live in a world that is sometimes sick and tired of *hearing* from Christians. What they need first is to *feel the love* of Christians. As Rosaria says, they might argue with our beliefs, "but who could argue with us *loving* them through genuine, mercy-driven hospitality?"[19]

CHAPTER | 17

When Heaven Gets Loud

No wise man, medium, magician, or
diviner is able to make known to the king
the mystery he asked about. But there is a
God in heaven who reveals mysteries.
—DANIEL 2:27–28 CSB

I was raised in a conservative, emotionally reserved, traditional Baptist home. Dreams, visions, and the interpretations thereof were not part of our standard spiritual repertoire. And yet the majority of Muslims I've personally seen come to faith in Christ did so, in part, through a supernatural vision.

At first I wasn't sure what to think about it—I certainly hadn't expected these things. But at this point I don't think I really have a choice of *not* believing in them.

When I lived in Southeast Asia, I got a call one night from a Christian friend who asked whether I could meet privately with one of his Muslim friends. We got together late one evening, and this thirty-two-year-old Muslim man, whom I'll call Mehmet, told me about a dream he'd had a month before. In the dream he'd found himself walking aimlessly through an expansive field. He walked for days and days, he said, feeling lost and alone. He knew this field represented his life.

Suddenly, he said, a voice from behind him called his name, and he turned to see a man in radiant white clothing with a face that shone like the sun. This messenger tried to hand him a copy of the *Injil* (the Muslim word for the Gospels), telling him that this was the only thing that would get him out of the field. Terrified, he refused, saying that as a Muslim he had no interest in the *Injil*. The dream abruptly ended, Mehmet said, and he woke up in a cold sweat, feeling as if he'd made a terrible mistake.

The next night he had the exact same dream. Same field, same strange Visitor, same offer. This time, however, he *wanted* to take the *Injil*, he just couldn't bring himself to do it.

The third night, Mehmet said, he was almost afraid to go to sleep. Sure enough, the moment he drifted off, he stood alone in the field with the Stranger. "This is the last time I will tell you this," the Stranger said. "This is the only thing that will get you out of this field." He held the *Injil* out to him again. Almost involuntarily, Mehmet said, his trembling hands reached out to take the book, and he pulled it to his chest. He awoke peacefully in his bed the next morning.

The man then looked at me and said, "My friend tells me you are an expert with *Injil*. Can you tell me what my dream means?"

Now, as I explained above, my little Baptist church didn't offer a class on dream interpretation. Still, in that moment, I am proud to report I knew exactly what to say! "Mehmet, my friend, you are so in luck! Dream interpretation is my spiritual gift!"

For the next couple of hours, I walked him through the whole Bible, both the Old and New Testaments, showing him how all prophets had told one big story about Jesus. At the end I asked him if he wanted to place his faith in Jesus. "With all my heart, yes," he said. I started to lead him through a traditional "sinner's prayer," but before we really got into it, I stopped.

I said, "Mehmet, I'm sorry. I just want to make sure you *know* what you are doing. I mean, this is a huge deal. You are becoming a follower of Jesus. We will need to follow this with baptism. And when that becomes public, you might lose your job. Your family may disown you. And we both know of people in this community who have *lost their lives* because they made this decision. I just want to make sure you are clear on what this might cost you."

Mehmet paused for a second, then smiled and said, "Of course I know this. Why do you think it took me a month to come and talk with you? In that month I decided that my visitor had to be Jesus, the main character of the *Injil*." He knew that Christians believed that Jesus was God come in the flesh to rescue us, and he decided that if that was true, and Jesus had appeared to him in this dream, there wasn't anywhere he wouldn't go with Jesus, regardless of what he had to leave behind.

Let me tell you: That kind of vision makes evangelism easy. Even in Babylon.

Missionaries to Muslim countries report these kinds of supernatural visitations with a significant degree of regularity, as do missionaries in many Buddhist, Hindu, and animistic places.[1] It seems that in places where the gospel is the least known, and the cost to follow Jesus so much steeper, God often adds a supernatural "signature" of sorts to help validate belief. We're never guaranteed this, of course, or told to demand it, but it does seem to happen a lot in difficult places.

That shouldn't be surprising. Daniel and the earliest Christians experienced this kind of validation in their respective Babylons, too. In fact, it was a key ingredient in their impact.

"There Is a God in Heaven"

Daniel 2 opens with Nebuchadnezzar waking up in a cold sweat. He'd had that dream again! Not a dream—a nightmare! So he did what he always did with confusing mysteries about the spirit world:

> The king gave orders to summon the magicians, mediums, sorcerers, and Chaldeans to tell the king his dreams. When they came and stood before the king, he said to them, "I have had a dream and am anxious to understand it." (Dan. 2:2–3 CSB)

Babylonian wise men had a little book with interpretive keys that helped explain what various elements in dreams meant. For example, cows meant prosperity; birds were a warning of danger; appearing before the royal court in nothing but your underwear meant you struggled with impostor syndrome and probably wet the bed as a kid. You know, standard stuff.

Using these images, the wise men would then concoct some interpretation of the dream, using very generalized terms, much like we'd see today in a horoscope or fortune cookie: "King, things are looking good for the next year," or "Don't trust friends who gossip about you," or something like that. Then they'd get paid the big bucks. Pretty easy gig.

But this time was different. The king, who apparently was no dummy, was so convinced that this dream was from the gods that he didn't want his wise men making up some interpretation like they usually did. So he added a caveat that would guarantee that any interpretation was actually from the gods. "First," he said, "you've got to tell me *what* the dream was. If you get that right, I'll know that your interpretation is also from the gods."

The wise men responded with bewilderment. "You are asking the impossible!" they said. "Never in the history of dream interpretation has any king required that from his wise men!" (vv. 10–11, my paraphrase). The king held firm, however, saying that if no wise men could tell him what his dream was, he'd know they were all impostors and would have the whole lot killed.

That's when Daniel stepped forward.

Daniel answered the king, "No wise man, medium, magician, or diviner is able to make known to the king the mystery he asked about. But there is a God in heaven who reveals mysteries." (vv. 27–28 CSB)

I love that phrase. *But there is a God in heaven.*

Daniel then correctly recounted Nebuchadnezzar's dream to him, in great detail, and gave the interpretation. The details of that particular dream aren't important to us right now; what's most significant is how Nebuchadnezzar responded:

> Then King Nebuchadnezzar fell upon his face and paid homage to Daniel, and commanded that an offering and incense be offered up to him. The king answered and said to Daniel, "Truly, your God is God of gods and Lord of kings, and a revealer of mysteries, for you have been able to reveal this mystery." Then the king gave Daniel high honors and many great gifts, and made him ruler over the whole province of Babylon and chief prefect over all the wise men of Babylon. (vv. 46–48)

Let's come back to the phrase "But there is a God in heaven who reveals mysteries." Daniel explained to Nebuchadnezzar that God was showing him who he was by doing things that only he could do. It was a divine affirmation of Daniel's testimony.

God sometimes puts his people into impossible situations *to show that there is a God in heaven.* Sometimes he does that by giving us codes to live by that set us apart; sometimes he does that by making us prosper as we abide by that code. Sometimes he does it through our indomitable joy in suffering or our refusal to compromise our convictions because of our certainty of a greater and more permanent treasure in him. Sometimes he does it through our radical generosity.

And sometimes he does it by breaking into an impossible situation by doing something only he can do. It's as if, through our humble, faithful obedience, heaven itself gets loud, punctuating our witness with a supernatural affirmation.

The early church experienced this fairly regularly in their own Babylons, too. The writer of Hebrews explained,

> [The gospel] was declared at first by the Lord [Jesus], and it was attested to us by those who heard [the apostles], while God also bore witness by signs and wonders and various miracles and by gifts of the Holy Spirit. (Heb. 2:3–4)

Paul said of his own ministry: "My speech and my preaching were not with persuasive words of wisdom but with a demonstration of the Spirit's power, so that your faith might not be based on human wisdom but on God's power" (1 Cor. 2:4–5 CSB). Paul didn't depend on human argumentation alone; he looked for supernatural validation. Paul said that in an ideal church service an unbeliever would have the secrets of his heart revealed through the supernatural gift of prophecy happening through believers. Then, aware that the believers are revealing things about him that only God could know, the unbeliever would fall on his face, worshiping God and acknowledging that God truly was among them (1 Cor. 14:25). Very Nebuchadnezzar-esque, if you ask me.

My wife, Veronica, experienced this as part of her own journey toward Christ. When she left for college, she was running from God. She reluctantly agreed to go to a beach weekend with some Christian friends. Upon getting there and finding out "worship sessions" were part of the weekend, she regretted her choice and tried her best to tune out the speakers. But at the end of one of the talks, the speaker asked attendees to pair up and pray for one another. Veronica said she was seated next to a girl she had never met, but as this girl prayed for her—a girl who knew literally nothing about her—she began to call out Veronica's fears, questions, and even her sins. She then prayed the love of God into her life. Veronica said the experience rattled her to her core; she felt completely exposed, absolutely sure she was in the presence of a God who was speaking *to her*. She went back to her hotel room broken, where she repented of her sin and turned control of her life over to God. God had given this girl words of knowledge about Veronica, which God used to make his reality known to Veronica's heart.

This was what Paul was describing in 1 Corinthians 14—supernatural experiences that *affirm* to unbelievers that there is a God in heaven. Loud affirmations. Again, not every person who comes to Christ has this kind of experience, but some do, and God seems to do it more in places where Christ is least known. By the way, if you're getting a little cynical right now, realize that this is not something only far-out, fringe Christians believe. The erudite Reformed Anglican Oxford PhD theologian J. I. Packer said,

> Prophecy [that is, revealing specific things pertinent to someone through the power of the Holy Spirit] has been and remains a reality whenever and where Bible truth is genuinely preached— that is, spelled out and applied, whether from a pulpit or more informally.[2]

I'm not sure exactly what this will look like in your secular Western workplace, but I'm quite sure, if the experience of the global church and the witness of Christian history are any indicators, we should expect more of these kinds of affirmations as Western culture becomes more "negative." Of course, this is not something you can weave into your "witness" strategy; God decides when and where he will do it. But don't be hesitant to ask him to do stuff like this, and don't be surprised when it happens.

God gives this kind of validation through more than just words of prophecy, too. The New Testament writer James said that God sometimes does it through miraculous answers to prayer. James pointed to the example of Elijah in 1 Kings: When Elijah wanted to prove to Israel who the true God was—Jehovah or Baal—the test he put forward was to see which God answered prayer. "You call upon the name of your god [Baal], and I will call upon the name of the LORD [Jehovah], and the God who answers . . . he is God" (1 Kings 18:24). The prophets of Baal danced and prayed for hours, to no avail, and then Elijah prayed a simple prayer and fire fell from heaven and consumed the altar Elijah had built even after he'd dumped gallons and gallons of water on it.

> And when all the people saw it, they fell on their faces and said, "The LORD, he is God; the LORD, he is God." (v. 39)

James then explained to us that, in the same way, "the prayer of a righteous person has great power as it is working" (James 5:16). Elijah was no different from us, James said. He wasn't some special breed of God follower with access to power none of us have access to anymore. Elijah simply perceived that God wanted to do something, asked him to do it, and God sent a miracle.

We can expect the same. James *commanded* us to expect the same.

One of our missionaries in South Africa recently told me this story:

> I got to see a Hindu-background Indian man come to faith after he lost everything in a bad business deal. When we met him, he thought God might be trying to speak to him, however. Over the next couple of days, he struggled with the idea that God could be all good and all powerful and let this tragedy befall him. Nevertheless, I felt compelled by the Holy Spirit to share with him the story of Elijah and the prophets of Baal, how God had demonstrated his reality by his ability to answer prayer. I then asked him if I could take a week to pray that in a similar way God would reveal himself to this man to be the one true God by

meeting some of his needs. So we prayed that the Lord would meet his need for new clothes. That very afternoon I got a random email from a church asking if we had any ministry needs because they had set some money aside specifically for us. We used the money to go to the mall to replace his entire wardrobe.

I asked at the end if I could pray for him. I prayed God's love over him and when I said "Amen," he asked if he could pray also. He said, "God, over the past week I had determined not to believe in you, and even considered ending my life. But today, through this answer to prayer, you have proven to me that you see and know me."

Perhaps this doesn't seem like too dramatic of an answer to prayer, one you might explain away as a coincidence. But when God is working in your life, he has a way of answering prayers that seems so directed and so intimate that you feel certain he is communicating with you. In what seems to others like just a random sound, you perceive a speaking voice (Acts 22:9).[3]

Are there places where you are giving God a chance to work like this? Maybe it starts by simply asking people at your workplace or in your neighborhood *how* you can pray for them. When I was a missionary in Southeast Asia, when I wasn't sure what else to do, I just offered to pray for people. I figured if I didn't know what to do, I should open the door for God to do what *he* wanted to do.

One of my favorite memories from my time over there was when five middle school boys showed up at my door one afternoon. I was several months into my time there and feeling pretty discouraged. No one seemed to be listening to me. My evangelistic conversations didn't seem to be going anywhere. Unsure of what else to do, I would take walks around my neighborhood, get into conversations with neighbors, and just ask them what I could pray for. I prayed for healing from sicknesses, guidance in decisions, and financial provision.

When I answered the door that afternoon, one of the boys said, "Mister, my mom is very sick. Can you come and pray for her?" I was shocked. Apparently so was one of the other boys in the group, because he said, "Why are you asking *him* to come pray? He's a Christian." "Yes," said the boy. "But God seems to listen to him."

I don't control what miraculous sign God provides or when he gives one, but what a reputation for us to have in Babylon! *The ones God listens to.*

Or as Nebuchadnezzar said to Daniel, "Truly, your God is God of gods and Lord of kings, and a revealer of mysteries, for you have been able to reveal this mystery" (Dan. 2:47).

The apostles assured us that this is the reputation God wants us to have. Jesus himself bid us to ask:

> "Until now you have asked nothing in my name. Ask, and you will receive, that your joy may be full." (John 16:24)

Don't write off God's heavenly affirmations as a thing of the past. Yearn for them. Ask for them. Receiving heavenly affirmation is part of what it means to shine like the stars in the sky. Supernatural signatures testify that there is a God in heaven—a God who is real, a God who loves and who listens, a God who is returning for his people.

So step out there and give God a chance to shine through you. Remember, thirty-nine of the forty miracles recorded in the book of Acts happened *outside* the church. We have not because we ask not.

Jesus commissioned us to show off God's salvation in Babylon, not to keep it hidden. Ask him for affirmations in the lives of the people you are trying to reach. Pray for opportunities to show that there is a God in heaven who does what no one else can do.

Putting him on display is why he has left you here in Babylon.

So as you honor Christ the Lord, live quietly and testify loudly. And ask God to back you up.

Testify through your faithfulness and excellence in small things. Testify through your courage. Testify through your generosity. Testify through your joy. Testify through the mind-boggling forgiveness and grace you extend. Testify through giving God a chance to work miraculously in and through you.

Shine, shine, shine.

"And those who are wise shall shine like the brightness of the sky above; and those who turn many to righteousness, like the stars forever and ever." (Dan. 12:3)

EPILOGUE

Maranatha

The year was 1861. Wilmer McLean was a fairly wealthy Virginian who owned a small farmhouse and a bunch of land just outside Manassas, Virginia. Tensions between North and South were high, and word on the street was that shots had been fired at Fort Sumter, South Carolina.

Wilmer McLean and his family were noncombatants, but that didn't stop Confederate general P. G. T. Beauregard from commandeering McLean's house to use as his headquarters for the First Battle of Bull Run—the battle historians regard as the first major land battle of the Civil War.

When the Union Army figured out that McLean's house was where the Confederate general's headquarters was, they shelled the house. One of their cannonballs even went down the chimney and exploded in the kitchen. And you thought hospitality made a mess in your house!

When the battle was over, McLean, who wanted no further part of the conflict, sold his land in Manassas and moved 120 miles southwest to another small sleepy village in Virginia called Appomattox.

You see where this is going?

Oh, it gets better.

The house McLean purchased in Appomattox served as the courthouse for the region, and four years later, on April 9, 1865,

Confederate general Robert E. Lee formally surrendered his armies to Union general Ulysses S. Grant in the parlor of Wilmer McLean's second house, effectively ending the Civil War.

That's right. In one of history's great ironies, the Civil War basically started and ended on the same guy's property, a guy who was trying his best to isolate himself from it.

Maybe you thought living quietly in Babylon meant distancing yourself from all conflict and pursuing a nice, comfortable life of peace, keeping your head down and minding your own business. Living quietly, however, is not a biblical strategy for running *from* the battle, it's one for running *into* it. It means living by different values, with different motivations, in pursuit of different goals. It means seeking to please a different Master and pursuing treasure in a different kingdom.

It means recognizing that some conflicts you can't stay neutral in.

It means getting up every day to go about your work, whether grandiose or mundane, and working with excellence, integrity, and generosity as a reflection of your King. It means standing for justice and shining as a bright gospel light in a dark political sky.

It means standing with unflinching courage in the face of even the fiercest opposition, knowing you have a King who has already walked through fire for you and come out unharmed, and who promises to go with you through every fire he sends you into. As the popular worship song says, we know "he stands by our side because he stood in our place."[1]

Living quietly means looking for opportunities to show off our King's incredible grace. It means having people who don't look like you or think like you or believe like you in your home and loving them like your King loves you.

And when God opens up a door for you to show off his grace, mercy, excellence, or power, do it boldly. Loudly. Your radical love, courage, joy, generosity, and hospitality will give you the opportunity to testify to the fact that there is a God in heaven.

The pastor who brought my family to Christ often ended our church services with the word "Maranatha." It means "Our Lord, come!" (1 Cor. 16:22).

Fittingly for us, it is an *Aramaic* word. It's from the language of Babylon.

So that's the Aramaic prayer I end this book with. May it become the anthem of your heart, the hope that shapes your vision to live quietly and testify loudly in Babylon.

Maranatha!

Even so come, King Jesus.

In the meantime, let's get busy being everyday revolutionaries.

By God's grace, we'll turn the world upside down just as Jesus' first followers did.

Against the world, for the world. The King is coming soon.

Notes

CHAPTER 1: JESUS IN THE PURPLE CITY

1. *Larry King Live*, "Should Christians Stop Trying to Convert Jews," aired January 12, 2000, on CNN.
2. Marvin Olasky, *Standing for Christ in a Modern Babylon* (Crossway, 2003), 13.
3. We have no written record of Athanasius saying these exact words. They are, however, a good summary of his overall missional approach. Christian theologians even today celebrate Athanasius with the phrase *Athanasius contra mundum* ("Athanasius against the world"). See "Athanasius Against the World," Ligonier, December 14, 2014, www.ligonier.org/learn /devotionals/athanasius-against-world.
4. N. T. Wright and Michael F. Bird, *Jesus and the Powers* (Zondervan, 2024), 7.

CHAPTER 2: LIFE IN THE MARGINS

1. *Silicon Valley*, episode 4, season 5, "Tech Evangelist," directed by Jamie Babbit, aired April 15, 2018, on HBO.
2. Francis A. Schaeffer, *The Great Evangelical Disaster* (Wheaton, IL: Crossway, 1984), 29.
3. Patricia Tevington, *Americans Feel More Positive Than Negative About Jews, Mainline Protestants, Catholics* (Pew Research Center, 2023), www .pewresearch.org/religion/2023/03/15/americans-feel-more-positive-than -negative-about-jews-mainline-protestants-catholics.
4. "Openness to Jesus Isn't the Problem—the Church Is," Barna, May 17, 2023, www.barna.com/research/openness-to-jesus.
5. Anugrah Kumar, "Andy Stanley Avoids Gay Issue in Last Sermon of Controversial Series," *Christian Post*, May 6, 2012, www.christianpost.com /news/pastor-andy-stanley-alludes-to-how-christians-should-treat-gays.html.
6. Alan Shlemon, "Homosexuality: Know the Truth and Speak It with Compassion," Stand to Reason, February 4, 2013, www.str.org/w /homosexuality-know-the-truth-and-speak-it-with-compassion.

Notes

7. Katherine Donlevy, "Apparent Drag 'Parody of Last Supper' at Paris 2024 Olympics Opening Ceremony Sparks Controversy," *New York Post*, July 26, 2024, https://nypost.com/2024/07/26/sports/drag-performers -seemingly-emulate-last-supper-at-olympic-opening-ceremony.

8. *Seinfeld*, season 4, episode 17, "The Outing," directed by Tom Cherones, aired February 11, 1993, on NBC.

9. Aaron M. Renn, "The Three Worlds of Evangelicalism," *First Things*, February 1, 2022, www.firstthings.com/article/2022/02/the-three-worlds -of-evangelicalism. The Supreme Court issued the *Obergefell* decision in 2014, saying that the Fourteenth Amendment requires all states to license marriages between same-sex couples and to recognize all such marriages. Renn (and many others) see this as a watershed moment in how the Christian worldview was regarded in public discourse.

10. Aaron Renn is correct, I believe, to say that the new "negative world" reality requires new approaches to missiology (the strategy for how to reach people). In the "positive world" the church often engaged in culture war (think Moral Majority) and the seeker-sensitive movement (think Bill Hybels and Rick Warren). In the "neutral" world we continued with the seeker-sensitive movement and added to it cultural engagement and communal chaplaincy. In the negative world, Renn says, these "missiologies" will no longer cut it.

11. Larry W. Hurtado, *Destroyer of the Gods: Early Christian Distinctiveness in the Roman World* (Waco, TX: Baylor University Press, 2016), especially chapter 1, "Early Christians and Early Christianity in the Eyes of Non-Christians."

12. Daniel 1:7; 4:8–9, 19; 10:1. In these passages, penned by Daniel himself, he accepted the name without apparent protest.

13. Tim Keller, "Born into Hope," sermon preached at Redeemer Presbyterian Church in Manhattan, New York, February 4, 2001, https://gospelinlife.com/sermon/born-into-hope/.

14. *Thayer's Greek Lexicon*, Electronic Database, 2011 by Biblesoft, Inc. Accessed via Bible Hub, https://biblehub.com/greek/2570.htm.

15. *Strong's Greek Lexicon*, "kalos," Bible Hub, https://biblehub.com /greek/2570.htm.

16. 1 Peter 2:13–16; 3:4, 9, 11, 15.

17. Jason Daye, host, *Frontstage Backstage*, podcast, "Compassion and Courage in Chaotic Times—Os Guinness," June 6, 2022, https://pastorserve.org /compassion-and-courage-in-chaotic-times-os-guinness.

18. John Mark Comer, *Practicing the Way: Be with Jesus, Become like Him, Do as He Did* (Waterbrook, 2024), 158.

19. Michael Green, *Evangelism in the Early Church*, rev. ed. (Eerdmans, 2003), 242–49.

Notes

CHAPTER 3: RIGHT WHERE WE'RE SUPPOSED TO BE

1. Jeremiah 25:11–12.
2. Cyrus's decree that the Jews should go home in Ezra 1:1–4 was seen as the fulfillment of the prophecies of Jeremiah 29:10–14 and Isaiah 44:28.
3. My paraphrase.
4. Henry T. Blackaby, Richard Blackaby, Claude V. King, *Experiencing God: Knowing and Doing the Will of God* (B&H, 2008), 56, 72.
5. Heather Holleman, Cru National Leadership Gathering, Milwaukee, WI, August 7, 2022.

CHAPTER 4: WHY ARE WE HERE?

1. Dawson Trotman, *Born to Reproduce* (NavPress, 2018).
2. Esau McCaulley, *Reading While Black: African American Biblical Interpretation as an Exercise in Hope* (IVP Academic, 2020), 94.
3. N. T. Wright and Michael F. Bird, *Jesus and the Powers* (Zondervan, 2024), 28, emphasis mine.
4. Wright and Bird, *Jesus and the Powers*, 28.
5. Wright and Bird, *Jesus and the Powers*, 29–30.
6. Wright and Bird, *Jesus and the Powers*, 26.
7. Os Guinness, *The Magna Carta of Humanity: Sinai's Revolutionary Faith and the Future of Freedom* (IVP, 2021); see also Guinness, *The Call: Finding and Fulfilling the Central Purpose of Your Life* (Nelson, 2003). These lines from the interview here: https://pastorserve.org /compassion-and-courage-in-chaotic-times-os-guinness/.
8. Tom Holland, *Dominion: How the Christian Revolution Remade the World* (Basic, 2019), 139–40. Holland's book is (probably) the most accessible and influential expression of this argument.
9. Holland, *Dominion*, 139.
10. Wayne Grudem and Barry Asmus, *The Poverty of Nations: A Sustainable Solution* (Crossway, 2013), 32.
11. "Girls' Education: Gender Equality in Education Benefits Every Child," UNICEF, https://www.unicef.org/education/girls-education/; "Gender Disparities in Education," June 2022, UNICEF, https://data.unicef.org /topic/gender/gender-disparities-in-education/.
12. Placide Cappeau, "O Holy Night" (1847).
13. McCaulley, *Reading While Black*, 53 (emphasis mine).
14. Martyn Lloyd-Jones, "The Parable of the Rich Fool: A Sermon on Luke 12:13–21," MLJ Trust, sermon, August 27, 1967, www.mljtrust.org /sermons/other-sermons/the-parable-of-the-rich-fool. See also Martyn Lloyd-Jones, *Studies in the Sermon on the Mount*: "The great doctrine of the soul must come first; the soul is greater than the body. We must never reverse the order."

15. The fact that Paul called those who disagreed with him "weak" (Rom. 14:2) indicates he was not unclear that he was right in this situation. In Romans 14:14, he said outright that his perspective was the correct one.

16. Laurie Goodstein, "Rev. Dr. Carl F. H. Henry, 90, Brain of Evangelical Movement," *New York Times*, December 13, 2003, https://www.nytimes .com/2003/12/13/us/rev-dr-carl-f-h-henry-90-brain-of-evangelical -movement.html.

17. Quoted in Andrea Palpant Dilley, "The Surprising Discovery About Those Colonialist, Proselytizing Missionaries," *Christianity Today*, January–February 2014, www.christianitytoday.com/2014/01/world -missionaries-made.

18. Quoted in Palpant Dilley, "Surprising Discovery."

19. Quoted in Palpant Dilley, "Surprising Discovery" (emphasis mine).

20. Several Bible scholars highlight this connection. For instance, Matthew Henry wrote, "We take God's name in vain . . . by hypocrisy, making a profession of God's name, but not living up to that profession"; Matthew Henry, *Commentary on the Whole Bible*, vol. 1, *Genesis to Deuteronomy*, commentary on Exodus 20:7, Christian Classics Ethereal Library, accessed January 23, 2025, www.ccel.org/ccel/henry/mhc1.Ex.xxi .html. As Kevin DeYoung explains, breaking the third commandment involves anything that profanes or devalues the name of God in the eyes of others; Kevin DeYoung, "What Does It Really Mean to Take the Lord's Name in Vain?" Crossway, October 24, 2018, www.crossway.org /articles/what-does-it-really-mean-to-take-the-lords-name-in-vain.

CHAPTER 5: IF YOU WANT TO MAKE A DIFFERENCE, YOU GOTTA BE DIFFERENT

1. Quoted in Elisabeth Elliot, *Shadow of the Almighty: The Life and Testament of Jim Elliot* (Authentic Classics, 2005), 79.

2. "Backmasking" meant recording a secret message into music (usually hard rock) backward so that it would be implanted in your brain without your knowing it. This was often presented as the primary way Satan was corrupting my generation.

3. Job and Noah are the other two (Ezek. 14:14).

4. We're not sure where Daniel was for this test. Some have suggested he was away on business or even up on the platform itself.

5. Revelation 2:12–17.

6. Dean M. Kelley, *Why Conservative Churches Are Growing: A Study in Sociology of Religion* (Mercer, 1996), 1.

7. Ryan Burge, "Why It's Unlikely U.S. Mainline Protestants Outnumber Evangelicals," Religion Unplugged, July 12, 2021, https://religionunplugged

.com/news/2021/7/12/why-its-unlikely-us-mainline-protestants
-outnumber-evangelicals.

8. "Episcopal Growth and Decline by the Numbers," Anglican Watch, August 27, 2023, www.anglicanwatch.com/episcopal-growth-and-decline -by-the-numbers.

9. Tim Keller, *The Decline and Renewal of the American Church* (Tim Keller and Gospel in Life, 2022), 4.

10. Michael Gryboski, "PCUSA Loses 1 Million Members in 15 Years: Report," *Christian Post*, December 4, 2024, www.christianpost.com /news/pcusa-loses-1-million-members-in-15-years-report.html.

11. Kelley, *Conservative Churches*, 20–21.

12. Kelley, *Conservative Churches*, 121.

13. Keller, *Decline*, 15.

14. Augustine of Hippo was North African by nationality and Berber-Roman by ethnicity.

15. Tim Keller, https://www.goodreads.com/quotes/408988-the-early-church -was-strikingly-different-from-the-culture-around. I've done a lot of digging in an attempt to find the original source for this, to no avail. At this point, it's most likely I heard this from one of his live sermons.

16. Larry Alex Taunton, *The Faith of Christopher Hitchens: The Restless Soul of the World's Most Notorious Atheist* (Thomas Nelson, 2016).

17. G. K. Chesterton, *The Everlasting Man* (World Invisible), pt. 2, chap. 6, www.worldinvisible.com/library/chesterton/everlasting/part2c6.htm (emphasis mine).

CHAPTER 6: AVOIDING THE CULTURE WAR DETOUR

1. Jeremiah 29:1–32.

2. Both Peter and John explicitly make the connection between our current living situation and Babylon in 1 Peter 5:13 and Revelation 14:8; 17:1–6, respectively.

3. John 18:36. Some have suggested that what Jesus really meant when he said, "My kingdom is not of this world," was that its *authority* was not of this world, and that he was saying his authority superseded Pilate's. That is certainly true, but his immediate application of his statement was that because his is not an earthly kingdom, his servants would not fight with earthly weapons to bring it in. He brings it; we are instruments of it and give signs and foretastes of it. Lesslie Newbigin, *The Gospel in a Pluralist Society* (Eerdmans, 1989).

4. Newbigin, *Gospel in a Pluralist Society*.

5. Quoted in Peter Wehner, "The Moral Universe of Timothy Keller," *Atlantic*, December 5, 2019, www.theatlantic.com/ideas /archive/2019/12/timothy-kellers-moral-universe/603001.

6. See, for example, the works of Jordan Peterson and Tom Holland. Where each of these men is on his faith journey is a fascinating question, but neither started his journey as a Christian apologist seeking to validate the Bible. Even many of the "new atheists" have softened their tone on Christianity. In 2024, Richard Dawkins stated, "Even as hostility toward Christianity and Christian morality has increased in recent years, a growing number of atheists, former atheists, and secularists verbalized the role Christianity played in shaping the Western world and why it is a necessary factor in preserving civilization"; John Stonestreet, "Christianity Is a Cultural Good," Breakpoint, December 30, 2024, https://breakpoint.org/christianity-is-a-cultural-good.

7. Michael Green, *Evangelism in the Early Church*, rev. ed. (Eerdmans, 2003), 168.

8. Tim Keller shared this with me in a private letter. It was the last one we exchanged before he died.

9. C. S. Lewis, "Faith," chap. 12 in *Mere Christianity* (HarperCollins, 2001).

10. Ephesians 5:11; Proverbs 31:8–9.

11. Although I am paraphrasing her words here, this was her sentiment. She was first interviewed in the *Durham Herald-Sun*. See more of her actual words here: "Church Efforts Earn Family Status at School," *Biblical Recorder* 175, no. 19 (September 12, 2009), 7. See also "Durham Names Principal of Year," WRAL News, November 2, 2007, https://www.wral.com/story/durham-names-principal-of-year/1997041/.

12. Acts 20:27–29; Ephesians 5:11–13.

13. This is my summary of Robert Lewis's strategy.

14. "Letter 22, to Arsacius, High-Priest of Galatia (c. 362 AD)," Tertullian Project, accessed October 22, 2024, www.tertullian.org/fathers/julian_apostate_letters_1_trans.htm.

15. Quoted in Marvin Olasky, *Standing for Christ in a Modern Babylon* (Crossway, 2003), 90.

16. John 1:14; 3:17.

17. We also can see the intimacy and tenderness with which Daniel and Nebuchadnezzar related to each other in passages like Daniel 4:19, "The king answered and said, 'Belteshazzar, let not the dream or the interpretation alarm you.' Belteshazzar answered and said, 'My lord, may the dream be for those who hate you and its interpretation for your enemies!'"

18. Matthew 5:13.

19. Olasky, *Standing for Christ in a Modern Babylon*, 149.

CHAPTER 7: RULES FOR PECULIAR PEOPLE POLITICS

1. I'm referring to things such as biblical principles of retributive justice, individual responsibility, the importance of private property ownership, and the need for checks and balances on power, given the

Notes

fallen nature of man; Wayne Grudem and Barry Asmus, *The Poverty of Nations: A Sustainable Solution* (Crossway, 2013).

2. Genesis 9:6.

3. This isn't the place to go into all the most relevant literature on gender, sexuality, and Scripture, so I'll offer just a few recommendations for further reading. Rob Smith's *How Should We Think About Gender and Identity?* helpfully offers a biblical overview as well as a history of the current transgender debate. Preston Sprinkle's *Embodied: Transgender Identities, the Church, and What the Bible Has to Say* is even more comprehensive, covering the same ground with biblical fidelity and heaps of grace. Both books acknowledge the small but not insignificant cases of mismatched genders, such as anatomical versus chromosomal anomalies, while providing a biblical and empathetic perspective on the contemporary gender conversation.

4. Romans 1:24–27.

5. Genesis 2:18–25; Romans 1:24–27.

6. Genesis 1:27; Acts 17:26; Romans 2:11.

7. Leviticus 19:9–10; Psalm 82:3–4; Proverbs 31:8–9.

8. The 2024 Democratic Party platform endorses, in no uncertain terms, abortion on demand. It says, "We believe unequivocally, that every woman should be able to access . . . safe and legal abortion." It also promotes that men and women can change their genders—for example, a boy who thinks he is a girl is, in fact, a girl. It goes on to say, "We will work to . . . guarantee transgender students' access to facilities based on their gender identity." https://democrats.org/wp-content/uploads/2024/09/2024_Democratic_Party_Platform_8a2cf8.pdf.

9. Luke 14:12–14; 1 John 3:17–18.

10. Arthur C. Brooks, *The Conservative Heart: How to Build a Fairer, Happier, and More Prosperous America* (Broadside, 2015).

11. For an analysis of the ideological roots behind critical theory and their deleterious effects on society, see Neil Shenvi and Pat Sawyer, *Critical Dilemma: The Rise of Critical Theories and Social Justice Ideology—Implications for the Church and Society* (Harvest House, 2023).

12. The "God Bless the USA Bible," first published in 2021, was promoted by Donald Trump during his 2024 presidential campaign. See https://godblesstheusabible.com.

13. For more of what Os Guinness has to say on this topic, see his book *The Call: Finding and Fulfilling the Central Purpose of Your Life* (Thomas Nelson, 2003), as well as his interview with Jason Daye, host, *Frontstage Backstage*, podcast, "Compassion and Courage in Chaotic Times—Os Guinness," June 6, 2022, https://pastorserve.org/compassion-and-courage-in-chaotic-times-os-guinness.

14. Carl Trueman, *The Rise and Triumph of the Modern Self: Cultural Amnesia, Expressive Individualism, and the Road to Sexual Revolution* (Crossway, 2020).
15. David Platt, *Before You Vote: Seven Questions Every Christian Should Ask* (Radical, 2020), 62–67. The examples are mine.
16. Abraham Kuyper, "The Church as Institution and as Organism," chap. 33 in *Common Grace: God's Gifts for a Fallen World*, ed. Jordan J. Ballor and Melvin Flikkema, vol. 2; most translators render Kuyper's alternative to "the church as organism" as "the church as institute."
17. Dietrich Bonhoeffer, as cited in Hannah Ward and Jennifer Wild, *The Lion Christian Quotation Collection* (BCA, 1997).

PART 2: LIVE QUIETLY (THE *KALOS* LIFE)

1. I have to thank my friend Ben Virgo, director of Christian Heritage Tours of London, England, for this excellent insight in a personal conversation.
2. A few have speculated about childhood miracles (for example, see Anne Rice, *Christ the Lord: Out of Egypt; A Novel* [Fawcett, 2006]), but they are based on mostly unreliable apocryphal sources.
3. "American Airlines Pilot Reportedly Promotes Christianity on Flight," Canadian HRReporter, February 9, 2004, www.hrreporter.com/news /hr-news/american-airlines-pilot-reportedly-promotes-christianity-on -flight/283846.
4. The most pivotal works in this vein are Lesslie Newbigin's *Foolishness to the Greeks: The Gospel and Western Culture* (Eerdmans, 1986) and *The Gospel in a Pluralist Society* (Eerdmans, 1991). But Newbigin's emphasis on a "missionary encounter with Western culture" pervades nearly every article and book he published.
5. Lesslie Newbigin, "Can the West Be Converted?" *International Bulletin of Missionary Research* 11, no. 1 (January 1987): 2–7.

CHAPTER 8: CREATION-FULFILLING

1. Tim Keller, *Every Good Endeavor: Connecting Your Work to God's Work* (New York: Penguin, 2014), 35, emphasis mine.
2. Martin Luther, "Small Catechism (1529)," in *The Book of Concord: The Confessions of the Evangelical Lutheran Church*, ed. Robert Kolb and Timothy J. Wengert, trans. Charles Arand (Fortress, 2000), 357–58.
3. Gene Edward Veith Jr., *God at Work* (Crossway, 2002), 13–14.
4. Kahlil Gibran, "On Work," Poets.org, https://poets.org/poem/work-4.
5. Jon Erlichman, "On this day in 1983: Apple recruited Pepsi's John Sculley to be its CEO. Steve Jobs famously asked him: 'Do you want to sell sugar water for the rest of your life, or do you want to

change the world?'" X, April 8, 2023, https://x.com/JonErlichman /status/1644695047562993665.

6. This is a fictional scene in the film, but it certainly represents Scottish Presbyterians' attitude toward work at the time.

7. I used these stories in my book *What Are You Going to Do With Your Life?* (B&H, 2020).

8. I owe this phrase to N. T. Wright, in *Simply Christian: Why Christianity Makes Sense* (HarperCollins, 2006).

9. C. S. Lewis, *The Last Battle* (HarperCollins, 1956), 228.

10. Jessilyn Lancaster, "Is This Billy Graham Prophecy About the Next Great Move of God Coming to Pass?" Charisma News, August 16, 2018, https://charismanews.com/marketplace/is-this-billy-graham -prophecy-about-the-next-great-move-of-god-coming-to-pass.

11. Tim Keller, *Center Church: Doing Balanced, Gospel-Centered Ministry in Your City* (Zondervan, 2012), 200. Or as the seventeenth-century politician Andrew Fletcher more cogently said, "Let me write the songs of a nation, and I care not who makes its laws"; Andrew Fletcher, "An Account of a Conversation Concerning a Right Regulation of Governments for the Common Good of Mankind (1703)."

CHAPTER 9: EXCELLENCE-PURSUING

1. Jennifer M. Wood, "15 Most Excellent Facts About Bill & Ted's Excellent Adventure," Mental Floss, August 28, 2020, www.mentalfloss.com /article/55079/15-things-you-might-not-know-about-bill-teds-excellent -adventure.

2. *Strong's Lexicon*, "yattir," Bible Hub, accessed February 28, 2025, https:// biblehub.com/hebrew/3493.htm.

3. Martin Luther King Jr., "Facing the Challenge of a New Age" (speech, First Annual Institute on Nonviolence and Social Change, Montgomery, Alabama, December 3, 1956), in *The Papers of Martin Luther King Jr.*, vol. 3, *Birth of a New Age, December 1955—December 1956*, ed. Clayborne Carson et al. (University of California Press, 1997).

CHAPTER 10: HOLINESS-REFLECTING

1. In such a case, shareholders make off with a substantial amount of profit, though the company declares bankruptcy, and the insured are left with nothing. Derivatives were a big factor in the economic crash of 2008.

2. Stephen Tomkins, *The Clapham Sect: How Wilberforce's Circle Transformed Britain* (Lion Hudson, 2010), 12.

3. Marvin Olasky, *Standing for Christ in a Modern Babylon* (Crossway, 2003), 13, 15.

Notes

CHAPTER 11: REDEMPTION-DISPLAYING

1. Tim Keller shared this story in a message I heard years ago. I have the notes from the sermon but not the location or date of hearing it!
2. I've heard Joby use this in multiple places, most recently in an interview with Josh Howerton, "Two Megachurch Pastors DEBUNK Megachurch Myths," *Resurge*, March 1, 2025, https://podcasts.apple.com/de /podcast/ep-10-two-megachurch-pastors-debunk-megachurch-myths /id1781083727?i=1000698223672.
3. "Reflections: First and Second Things," C. S. Lewis Institute, July 1, 2017, https://www.cslewisinstitute.org/resources/reflections-july-2017. My paraphrase.

CHAPTER 12: MISSION-ADVANCING

1. "The 10/40 Window," Window International Network, https://www .win1040.org/about-the-1040-window.
2. "About Three-in-Ten U.S. Adults Are Now Religiously Unaffiliated," Pew Research Center, December 14, 2021, https://www.pewresearch.org/religion/2021/12/14 /about-three-in-ten-u-s-adults-are-now-religiously-unaffiliated/.
3. Mike Barnett, *Discovering the Mission of God: Best Missional Practices for the 21st Century* (IVP Academic, 2012).
4. Bahram Khodabandeh, "Number Crunching: The Truth Behind Iran's 'Single-Digit' Unemployment Rate," Iran Wire, May 14, 2021, https://iranwire.com/en/features/69545/.
5. G. Kittel, G. W. Bromiley, and G. Friedrich, eds., *Theological Dictionary of the New Testament* (Eerdmans, 1964).
6. NAMB Staff, "Engaging Public Schools," North American Mission Board, https://www.namb.net/resource/engaging-public-schools/.

CHAPTER 13: LOUD COURAGE

1. C. S. Lewis, *Screwtape Letters* (Macmillan, 1977), 137.
2. Albert Mohler, "The Briefing," February 8, 2021, https://albertmohler .com/2021/02/08/briefing-2-8-21.
3. Alexei Navalny, *Patriot: A Memoir*, trans. Arch Tait and Stephen Dalziel (Knopf, 2024).
4. Daniel 2:25–29, 46–49.
5. Scott Scruggs, "Truth or Tolerance," Probe Ministries International, 1996, https://www.leaderu.com/orgs/probe/docs/truthtol.html.
6. Tim Keller, "Exclusivity: How Can There Be Just One True Religion?," sermon, Redeemer Presbyterian Church, September 24, 2006, https:// www.youtube.com/watch?v=75qetP4dRAA. "One of the great

paradoxes of history is the fact that when Christianity began to grow in the earliest days, the Greeks and the Romans had what looked like inclusive theology. They said, 'Everybody's got a god, you've got a god, I've got my god, they've got their god, nobody has theirs. There's no god for everybody. Everybody has their own god.' That was the Greco-Roman paganism."

7. Becket Cook, *A Change of Affection: A Gay Man's Incredible Story of Redemption* (Thomas Nelson, 2019).

8. Esau McCaulley, *Reading While Black: African American Biblical Interpretation as an Exercise in Hope* (IVP Academic, 2020), 34.

9. This quote is often attributed to Martin Luther, but its exact origin is uncertain. It certainly aligns with Luther's teachings on steadfastness, but there is no definitive evidence that he authored this specific phrase. It's possible that the quote has been paraphrased or perhaps used to summarize Luther.

CHAPTER 14: LOUD JOY

1. David Platt, "Living in Light of Eternity, Part 2: How Do You Press on in Difficult Days," sermon, McLean Bible Church, Vienna, Virginia, August 15, 2021.

2. By the way, according to the Siddur, the first-century Jewish prayer book, every morning Jewish men would thank God that they were not "a woman, a slave, or a Gentile." Get your mind around this. The first church service in Philippi would have included a woman, a slave, a Gentile, and a former Jewish religious leader!

3. Tim Keller (@TimKellernyc), X.com, June 23, 2024, https://x.com/timkellernyc/status/1804914830416945340.

CHAPTER 15: LOUD GENEROSITY

1. See Rodney Stark, *The Rise of Christianity* (HarperCollins, 1997), 161, 163–67.

2. Julian, *Epistola Nr. 39*, in B. K. Weis, *Julian: Briefe* (Heimeran, 1973).

3. From Eberhard Arnold, ed., *The Early Christians: In Their Own Words* (Plough, 1970), 14 (emphasis mine).

4. Scott Barkley, "Georgia Church Gives Nearly $25K to Erase More Than $5.7M in Medical Debt," *Baptist Press*, January 6, 2025, https://www.baptistpress.com/resource-library/news/georgia-church-gives-nearly-25k-to-erase-more-than-5-7m-in-medical-debt/.

5. Francis A. Schaeffer, *The Mark of the Christian* (InterVarsity Press, 1970), 29.

6. Beth Moore was another focus of his attacks. I beat her out for Worst Christian of 2019 by just a few points! Sorry, Beth!

Notes

7. The quoted material that appears has been saved here: https://drive
.google.com/file/d/1zvW—DRmfLT251cr860Y_ZMfL86XiKbz/view.

CHAPTER 16: LOUD HOSPITALITY

1. Rosaria Champagne Butterfield, "My Train Wreck Conversion,"
Christianity Today, January–February 2013, https://www
.christianitytoday.com/2013/02/my-train-wreck-conversion/.
2. Rosaria Champagne Butterfield, *The Secret Thoughts of an Unlikely
Convert: An English Professor's Journey into Christian Faith* (Crown &
Covenant, 2012), 14.
3. Robert J. Karris, *Eating Your Way Through Luke's Gospel* (Liturgical,
2006).
4. Tim Chester, introduction to *A Meal with Jesus: Discovering Grace,
Community, and Mission Around the Table* (IVP, 2013).
5. John Mark Comer, *Practicing the Way: Be with Jesus, Become like Him, Do
as He Did* (Waterbrook, 2024), 145.
6. Robert J. Karris, *Luke: Artist and Theologian* (Wipf & Stock, 2008), 47
(emphasis mine).
7. Comer, *Practicing the Way,* 206.
8. Rosaria Butterfield, *The Gospel Comes with a House Key: Practicing
Radically Ordinary Hospitality in Our Post-Christian World* (Crossway,
2018), 95.
9. Christine Pohl, *Making Room: Recovering Hospitality as a Christian
Tradition* (Eerdmans, 1999), 31.
10. For more on God taking our treatment of the poor personally, see James
2:14–16 (which says that treatment of the poor is a litmus test for our
faith's legitimacy) or Amos 2:6–7; 4:1; 8:4–6.
11. Butterfield, *Gospel Comes with House Key,* 228.
12. Lance Ford and Brad Brisco, *Next Door as It Is in Heaven: Living Out
God's Kingdom in Your Neighborhood* (NavPress, 2016), 100.
13. Ford and Brisco, *Next Door as It Is in Heaven,* 101.
14. Adapted from David Platt in a message I heard him give overseas to a
group of college students.
15. Butterfield, *Gospel Comes with House Key,* 111.
16. Butterfield, *Gospel Comes with House Key,* 125.
17. Ford and Brisco, *Next Door as It Is in Heaven,* 102.
18. Talk given at Summit Church in 2012. See also https://vergenetwork
.org/2011/11/14/6-ways-to-live-your-life-on-mission-jeff-vanderstelt
-video/.
19. Butterfield, *Gospel Comes with House Key,* 95, emphasis mine.

CHAPTER 17: WHEN HEAVEN GETS LOUD

1. J. Dudley Woodberry, Russell G. Shubin, and G. Marks, "Why Muslims Follow Jesus," *Christianity Today*, October 2007, https://www.christianitytoday.com/2007/10/why-muslims-follow-jesus/. This study was conducted between 1991 and 2007, interviewing 750 Muslims who have decided to follow Christ. The respondents were from thirty countries and fifty ethnic groups, representing every major region of the Muslim world. See also Warrick Farah, "Emerging Missiological Themes in MBB Conversion Factors," *International Journal of Frontier Missiology* 30, no. 1 (Spring 2013): 13–20. A pretty extensive list of studies is included in this article, showing the common themes for Muslim-background believers—with dreams and visions being a prominent recurring theme.

2. J. I. Packer, *Keep in Step with the Spirit: Finding Fullness in Our Walk with God* (Baker, 2005), 174.

3. On the road to Damascus, Paul says the men traveling with him saw the light and heard a sound, but only he perceived the voice speaking to him (Acts 9:7; 22:9).

EPILOGUE: MARANATHA

1. "You stand by my side / And You stood in my place / Jesus no other name." "Worthy of Your Name," Passion Worship, 2017.